START AND RUN A PROFITABLE CRAFT BUSINESS

START AND RUN A PROFITABLE CRAFT BUSINESS
A complete step-by-step business plan

William G. Hynes

Self-Counsel Press
(a division of)
International Self-Counsel Press
Canada   U.S.A.

Printed in Canada

First edition: April, 1984
Second edition: July, 1986
Reprinted: March, 1987; May, 1987; September, 1987; April, 1988; September, 1988; December, 1988; May, 1989; December, 1989

Cataloguing in Publication Data
Hynes, William G.
    Start and run a profitable craft business
    (Self-counsel series)
    ISBN 0-88908-644-3

1. Handicraft — Management. 2. Handicraft — Marketing. 3. Selling — Handicraft.
I. Title.   II. Series.
HD2341.H95   1986   745.5'068   C86-091332-5

The crafts in cover photo are courtesy of Circle Craft Gallery Shop, 328 Water Street, Vancouver, British Columbia, V6B 1B6

A Wonderland "Amy Doll" is courtesy of Queensdale Shop, 3010 Lonsdale, North Vancouver, British Columbia, V7N 3J5

Self-Counsel Press
(a division of)
International Self -Counsel Press Ltd.
Head and Editorial Office
1481 Charlotte Road
North Vancouver, British Columbia V7J 1H1

U.S. Address
1704 N. State Street
Bellingham, Washington   98225

CONTENTS

LIST OF SAMPLES

1

THE ADVANTAGES OF A CRAFT BUSINESS

A successful craft business can be started and operated by almost anyone who is prepared to follow the suggestions in this book. If you are already involved in crafts, then you have a good head start. But even if you have never produced a handcrafted product, you can still learn to set up and operate a successful craft business.

One man, bored and frustrated with a dead-end job, turned his woodworking hobby into a profitable business that now provides full-time employment for himself and an assistant.

A housewife and mother of two small children wanted to do something in addition to looking after her children. She did not want to go to work for someone else, especially since she had no specific job training except as a secretary, a job she had always disliked.

Then one day she had a brilliant idea. She had always enjoyed designing and making clothes for her own children, and she thought that just for fun she would try selling some of her work in a local craft market. Now, two years later, she has built up a successful part-time business making handcrafted children's clothes. Her part-time business brings in more money than she earned as a full-time secretary and it allows her to be at home with her children as well.

These two people love their work and by properly organizing the business side of their crafts, they are making good profits at the same time. What more could one want?

There are several hundred thousand craftworkers in the U.S. and Canada affiliated with craft organizations. It is estimated that there are at least as many who do not belong to an organization. These craftworkers range from individuals who earn extra income from their part-time business to designer-craftspeople who own and manage substantial companies and direct the work of highly skilled employees.

The technical efficiency of our modern society and its cheap, mass market products with their built-in obsolescence has created a large and growing consumer craving for finely wrought, individually produced, handmade products. Each year billions of dollars worth of handcrafted products are sold in North America, and the market is growing rapidly.

Most of these products are made by individual craftworkers and small to medium craft companies. Most of them work out of their own homes. They usually started their craft businesses in their spare time, so there was no need for them to give up their jobs until their businesses were off and running.

One of the biggest advantages of a craft business is that it can be started at home in your spare time. There is no need to invest in a costly plant and equipment. Most handcrafted products are made with the simplest of tools and equipment, rarely costing more than a few hundred dollars and in many cases much less.

Your initial workplace can be your garage or basement or even your kitchen. Most crafts are relatively clean and quiet, involving no personal health or environmental hazards. The level of skill required varies widely, but most craft skills can be easily acquired by a person of average intelligence and manual dexterity.

Craftworkers are made, not born. In the past, they learned from their parents, and skills were often handed down from generation to generation. Today, most craftspeople learn their skills by self study, by taking craft courses, or from a friend.

Large numbers of people are already good amateur craftworkers. Think of the vast number of men and women who make, usually as a hobby or a way of saving money, handcrafted sweaters, socks, furniture, toys, and thousands of other items. These people may not think of themselves as craftworkers, though they already have many of the skills required to start a successful craft business.

Even if you are not now making anything, you are still able to train yourself as a craftworker. The list of possible handcrafted products is so extensive and the levels and types of skills required so varied that it is hard to imagine anyone who is not capable of making something handcrafted, and with the help of this book, turning it into a marketable product.

In fact, this book will show you how to start out no matter what stage you have already reached. It covers such topics as how to acquire the skills you need, identify a marketable product, set up a production crafts workshop, and above all how to make your business profitable and achieve financial independence.

The value of financial independence has never been greater. Inflation, high unemployment, and general economic uncertainty are going to be with us in the foreseeable future. Rapidly changing technology is making many jobs redundant, and more and more people are succumbing to a feeling that their lives are being altered by economic forces they can neither understand nor control.

A craft business can give you a great measure of personal independence. You can be free of the nine to five grind, the pressures of cranky bosses and unpleasant co-workers, and the constant threat of lay-off. You can be your own boss and set your own working hours and conditions. You can make substantial profits.

In addition to all this, a craft business gives you the chance to express yourself creatively, turning out high quality, aesthetically appealing products.

But you don't have to be a creative genius to start a craft business. In fact, you don't even need to be particularly creative. Many successful craftworkers produce all their work according to traditional designs. Others modify traditional designs to serve their own purposes.

You can produce hundreds or thousands of "production line" crafts, (i.e., multiple copies) of the same design. Or you can concentrate on making one-of-a-kind craft pieces, where each piece is a unique design.

There are good markets for both kinds of products in just about any craft medium. Whether you want to work in wood, clay, fibre, glass or any one of hundreds of natural or synthetic materials, the markets for good quality handcrafted products are large and growing.

2

HOW TO GET STARTED

Perhaps you are already making handcrafted products as a hobby and you want to make your hobby into a business. Or perhaps you have had no previous involvement in crafts, but have experience in some other kind of business. You will have already acquired some of the knowledge and skills necessary to set up a successful craft business.

But what if you have never made anything handcrafted? What if you have had no previous business experience of any kind? What are your chances of successfully setting up and operating your own craft business? Your chances are as good as anyone else's. If you are prepared to work hard at mastering the techniques of your chosen craft and if you go about the business side of it in a professional way, you are almost certain to succeed.

Suppose you are already involved in pottery, for example, as a hobby. Chances are that you will want to make pottery in your craft business. Perhaps you consider your level of skills sufficiently advanced for you to begin marketing your work right away. You want to turn your hobby into a business. You can skip the rest of this chapter if you wish and go right to chapter 3.

While this chapter is intended mainly for someone who is starting out right from the beginning, it can still be read to advantage by the practicing amateur craftsperson.

a. WHAT TO MAKE

Even though you have no previous experience in crafts, you may have quite definite ideas about what interests you. If you feel a strong attraction to any particular medium, e.g., leather, stone, wood, then that's the place to start. Or perhaps you are more interested in making specific objects, e.g., clothing, toys, tableware, but have no really clear idea about a medium.

If certain types of handcrafted products have a special appeal to you, or if you feel that you have a special flair for something, that's the obvious place to start. There are opportunities of selling your work in most of the traditional and contemporary craft fields.

If you have no previous craft experience and haven't the faintest idea of where to start, make a list of your skills or talents, your hobbies, and your job experience. You'll very likely discover that you are more versatile than you originally thought.

Think of the things you've built in your basement workshop: the furniture for the children's rooms, the plywood runabout you made last winter, and all the other bits and pieces you've made for the house. You've always liked working with wood in your spare time. With a little more experience, you could make almost anything in wood.

Or perhaps you enjoy knitting and crocheting and are pretty good at it. Think of all the things you make for the children or as Christmas gifts for friends and relatives. Why not try offering some of your handknitted sweaters for sale? You've seen similar products in craft shops at prices of anywhere from $50 to $150, and many of them were not half as nice as yours.

If you've never made anything at all, think of some of the things you'd like to make and try them out. Start out with what interests you the most. If you think you'd like making jewelry or hooking rugs, then start there. Look around at craft markets and in craft shops for products you think you would like to make or learn to make.

Browse through some of the many craft books available. There are literally thousands of books on crafts and most likely your public library or nearby bookstore has a good selection. If you don't have any particular craft in mind, then get one of the A to Z books on the various kinds of handcrafted products being made in North America. Look at both traditional and modern crafts.

Perhaps you might want to enroll in a craft course. The availability of craft courses in your area can usually be determined by contacting your regional crafts organization (see Appendix 1). In some cases, craft courses are put on by local crafts organizations in your community.

Once you find the particular field that interests you, you'll want to know how you can go about learning the skills you'll need.

b. HOW TO LEARN CRAFT SKILLS

Your goal is to achieve a mastery of the craft you have chosen. This is not something you will accomplish overnight. As your skills improve, you will set new challenges for yourself, and practicing your craft will become an ongoing learning process.

This does not mean that you must study and practice for years before you can sell any of your work. On the contrary, if you have chosen a field in which you are particularly adept, you can produce marketable work within a short period of time. In most craft fields, you can start marketing your work while you are learning. You will naturally begin producing simpler pieces first, following traditional or already popular contemporary designs. You should not strive for too much originality at this point, but try to master basic techniques.

Craft skills can be learned the same way most other skills are. There are a number of different ways of learning, none of which is inherently better than any other. Try the one that appeals most to you. Or try them all.

1. Courses

There is a widespread belief today that you cannot really know anything about a subject unless you have taken a course in it. This is, of course, utter nonsense. Craft courses have a valid place in the learning process, but they are far from being the only route to mastery of a craft.

Craft instruction is available in most larger towns and cities. Formal craft study can go all the way from community evening courses at the local high school to the level of a university degree program. There are courses for the beginner and advanced courses for experienced craftworkers. (Many universities in the United States are now offering a master's degree in crafts.) Contact your local, state or provincial crafts organization for information on the availability of craft courses in your community.

But, wait a minute, you say, I want to start making things, not go through a 12-month course, let alone a university crafts program. I want to set up a craft business, not enroll in a course of study.

You're perfectly right. There's no reason why you have to complete a formal training course at all. Formal training in a craft, whether a single course or a whole program of courses, is in itself no guarantee that you will master the craft. Courses also have very little to do with the degree of commercial success you will have. Some of the best professional craftworkers around are entirely self-trained.

Whether or not you choose to take a craft course is very much a question of preference, depending partly on your own skills and partly on how you think you can best learn something new. Let's look at the other ways of learning.

2. Apprenticeship

Perhaps you would rather work on a one-to-one basis with a professional craftworker. There are professional, working craftspeople who will provide apprenticeship training in their own studios. Some charge fees for the instruction; others offer training in return for help in their business. This can be an excellent way of learning about production as well as marketing and other aspects of a craft business.

Apprenticeship training can provide you with valuable insights into the nature of your craft that are almost impossible to get otherwise. If your instructor is really good, the creative inspiration you receive can have a major influence on your whole subsequent career. Your reputation can be greatly enhanced by having been an apprentice of someone who is widely known and respected in a particular field.

Unfortunately, opportunities for this kind of training are few. Most commercial craftworkers are too busy to provide training for an apprentice. Those who do usually accept only one apprentice at a time. Some craftworkers may be reluctant to provide training to someone whose main goal is to set themselves up in their own business in the same area.

If you are interested in this kind of training, you may have to travel to another part of the country. But it's worthwhile if you get the opportunity to learn firsthand from a professional who is tops in his or her field.

Your local or regional crafts organization may have a list of the names of craftspeople who are willing to take on apprentices. Or, if you know a professional whose work you admire, you may want to approach him or her and ask to be taken on as an apprentice.

3. Teaching yourself

Perhaps you would rather teach yourself the skills you need. Many craftworkers have learned this way. Even if you have undergone formal training, you will find that the only way you can perfect the skills you have learned is by practice.

Books are an invaluable source of information on techniques, products, ideas, and markets. But don't just read; try out the techniques and experiment with the methods described. You don't have to read a book from cover to cover for it to be of use to you. Get in the habit of using books to dig out just the specific information you require.

No matter how you go about it, you will learn most about your chosen craft by actually doing it. Follow closely the techniques that you have read about or that you have learned from your instructor or craftworker friend. Don't expect to produce a masterpiece at the very outset. Chances are you'll spoil some materials in the beginning and make a bit of a mess without having a lot to show for it. Don't be discouraged. Keep trying. If you've chosen something that you like, the learning process can be a lot of fun. As you make progress, you'll be rewarded by the feeling of satisfaction and accomplishment that comes from creating something.

You have now taken the first big step on the way to setting up your own craft business. The next chapter will tell you how to make things that will sell.

3

HOW TO MAKE THINGS
THAT WILL SELL

Whether you are teaching yourself or taking a course, you will experiment a lot on your own, testing new techniques, investigating new materials, and learning new skills. You will experience one of humanity's oldest and most deeply ingrained urges, the desire to create — to make with your own hands an object that has both an aesthetic and a functional value. Whether you're making hand-dipped candles or jade pins, the feeling of satisfaction from creating is the same.

This is all very fine, you say, but what about business? You're not making crafts just for the feeling of self-fulfillment that you get. You want to make some money at it too.

This is where you differ from most of the people who become casually involved with crafts. Most of those in your pottery or ceramics course, for example, want to make pots or paint figurines for relaxation or as a hobby. You are taking up pottery or ceramics with the intention of starting a business and selling your work at a profit.

Whether you're going to learn metal-working or quilt-making or whatever as a pleasant way to pass the time or in order to make products to sell, you still have to master the basic techniques of the craft. There's no real difference there. The important difference between the professional and the amateur or hobbyist is in the way you select and design the particular products you make. For example, if you're involved in woodworking as a hobby, you can make what you please. If you fancy making elaborate sideboards and other big pieces, that's fine. But if you plan to sell your work, you have to follow the market. You won't make any money producing big, one-of-a-kind items, *no matter how nice they are*, if people are chiefly interested in buying small, less expensive pieces like cheeseboards or spice racks.

This applies no matter what stage you have reached in your craft career or what kind of products you are making. A number of friends of mine were formerly enthusiastic amateurs, producing work chiefly for their own pleasure, before they turned to crafts to make a living. In each case, they have had to substantially modify the products they were making in order to make their work marketable on a significant commercial scale.

In some cases, it may be necessary to make a radical change in the products you make if you want to be successful in the marketplace. This happened to Arthur and Betty Allthumbs. They wanted to establish a business making handcrafted furniture. They started out by making elaborate pieces like sideboards and chests with carved oak panels. Their work was extremely impressive and beautifully done. It got a lot of attention at craft shows, but few buyers.

Arthur and Betty made numerous efforts to promote their work. They exhibited frequently, had brochures printed, and set off their displays with attractive props, including flowers, vases, and stuffed toys. Still they sold only a few pieces here and there, not enough to make a living from their craft. Worse, from Arthur's point of view, was that people kept wanting to buy their "lovely" props, especially the stuffed toys that Betty made to advertise their work. Finally, they realized they had been ignoring a good opportunity.

Betty increased the number and variety of toys she made. It was not long before Arthur's carved chests and sideboards became booth fixtures for displaying the stuffed toy animals. Soon, Arthur joined forces with his wife to produce the new product line. Within a short time, the couple built up a substantial business producing handmade stuffed toys.

IF YOU WANT TO MAKE ANY MONEY SELLING YOUR WORK, YOU HAVE GOT TO PRODUCE WITH YOUR EYES FIXED FIRMLY ON THE MARKET. You must have a quality product to begin with, but you must also produce what is marketable if you expect to make a living from your craft.

You don't usually have to go to the extreme of switching to a completely different medium as Arthur and Betty did. There will be a market for your work in virtually any of the main craft categories, provided you are producing the right product. But in order to do this you first have to test the market.

a. MARKET RESEARCH

You may think market research is only for big companies with big budgets, while all you want to do is sell a few pots, or handknitted sweaters. You can go ahead and sell a few pots or handknitted sweaters and not bother about researching the market. But if you really want to sell significant quantities of a product and make substantial profits, you have to know the market, i.e., what people want to buy.

Your research need not be expensive or time-consuming. You will certainly find it worth the time and effort to find out what you can about potential markets before you start producing goods for sale.

Aim to find out as much of the following as you can:

(a) What are the possible retail outlets in your immediate area? (Look at chapter 7 on marketing for the different types of stores that carry handcrafted products.)

(b) Who are the typical customers of these shops? What are their approximate income levels? Are they mainly men or women? If, for example, you are producing clothing accessories like scarves and handbags, you would expect to be selling mainly to women.

(c) Is there a significant tourist trade in the area or do the stores cater chiefly to the area's residents? If tourists are important, try to think of products that may easily be identified with the area, e.g., products with a nautical theme are usually popular with tourists in coastal areas.

(d) What kinds of prices are being paid for products similar to the ones you plan to make? How important a factor is price? A few handmade products are true luxury items and price is not a major factor in determining whether they will sell. But most products are more price sensitive.

(e) Is your type of product affected by fashion? Most clothing items are.

(f) How much competition is there? Have your competitors been around for long? If there is a lot of well-established competition, you may be better off staying away from that product and making something different.

b. MARKET TEST YOUR PRODUCTS

Build prototypes of the products you plan to make and check your market research by actually testing your products in the market. You can use any of the marketing channels outlined in chapters 4 to 6 to do this, but selling the products at a craft market is one of the best.

Selling at a craft market gives you firsthand knowledge of customers' reactions to your products. What do they think of the quality of your work? Are your prices considered to be high or low? Are they looking for work similar to yours but perhaps in slightly different sizes, styles or colors?

Make prototypes using your existing facilities as much as possible, even if this means working on the top of the kitchen table in the beginning. Once you have discovered what is going to sell, you can start building up a stock of products, set up an adequate workshop, buy raw materials in bulk, and follow the other production techniques of a craft business as outlined in chapters 8 and 9. Don't put the cart before the horse and invest time, money, and effort in building up a stock of goods for which there is no market.

Try to find your own particular niche in the market. Look at what is selling in stores and at craft markets. Look at the quality and the prices. Concentrate on products that are in demand and that you can offer in a better design, quality or price.

Say you are producing wooden toys and there are lots of similar products in stores but they are almost all relatively large softwood toys. You may find a comfortable niche in the market by producing small, brightly painted hardwood toys for under $5.

Be careful to exhibit and offer for sale only your best work. Nothing travels faster than bad news, and you don't want your reputation to be based on premature work. If you are making production line crafts, one of the main skills you will develop is the ability to produce rapidly at a high standard of quality. But do not try to produce work quickly in the beginning.

Be prepared to follow the market and produce work for which there is a strong demand. The market for crafts is growing very quickly for those who are producing the right quality crafts. You will succeed if your work is of consistently high quality, if you follow the market to know what is selling, and if you know where to sell. Chapters 4 to 7 show you how to market your work.

4

WHOLESALE OR RETAIL?

How do you go about finding a market for your work? Once you have identified and produced a marketable product, choosing your market is the most important decision you will make. Unless you can find markets, your work won't be sold, and while you may enjoy making crafts, you won't make any money and you won't be in business for long.

In marketing your work, you leave the ranks of the amateurs and become a true professional. This important transition is marked by a change in attitude toward your work. In the beginning, the objects you made were worthwhile because "you" made them, and you were naturally very proud of the fact. At the same time, you hoped that others would also find your work attractive. You might have shown the work to your craft instructor, a friend or a fellow craftworker. As a professional, you retain this basic pride in your work, but at the same time you come to regard the product less as an extension of yourself and more as an object in the marketplace. It is a beautiful object, to be sure, the result of your painstaking efforts, but you now come to see it as a high quality, well-priced and marketable product.

Your task now is to take this product and sell it!

a. WHOLESALE VERSUS RETAIL

There are two basic ways you can go about selling your work. You can retail your products directly to the public or you can wholesale them to shops. Each method has its advantages and disadvantages. They are not mutually exclusive, and most successful craftworkers are involved to varying degrees in both wholesale and retail sales of their work.

1. Selling to stores

If you sell your work outright to stores, you get on average about half the final selling price. This is because most stores will mark up your goods by 100%, that is, they will sell your work at double the price you sell to them. This may seem excessive, but you must remember that retailers have big expenses, including high rents and taxes. If they are to be successful, they must be in a good location and spend money on advertising. No matter what they do a certain amount of merchandise is always going to remain unsold and they have to absorb the loss.

It is possible to deal with some stores on a consignment basis. In this arrangement, the store does not actually purchase your work but agrees to put it on display and sell it for you. If you deal with a shop on this basis, you should get a higher proportion of the final selling price, between 60% and 70%, because the risk is yours, not theirs. If you deal on a consignment basis, you should have a written agreement with the shop; see the section on contracts in chapter 10.

You may be obliged to sell to shops on consignment at the beginning of your career. If your work is unknown, store owners may be unwilling to run the risk of outright purchase. However, as soon as your work becomes accepted in the marketplace, you should insist on a straight sale in dealing with most shops.

Consignment is an unwieldy arrangement at best, as you never know exactly how much work you have sold until the retailer sends you your payment at the end of the month. Also, the retailer does not have the same incentive to promote your work if he or she has not invested any money in it.

Moreover, consignment involves considerably more paperwork than a straight sale. In addition to a written agreement with the consignee (see chapter 10), you need to keep detailed records of how much of your stock is in the hands of the consignee at the end of each month.

It is possible to sell to shops on a strictly cash basis, but as we shall see in a later chapter, this can hurt your sales if your competitors or other craftworkers are selling their goods on credit. In most cases, it will be necessary to offer your work on credit if you have any substantial amount of dealings with shops.

2. Retailing your own work

If you sell directly to the public, you receive all of the final selling price yourself. But then you have to reckon on *your* retail selling expenses before you start counting your profits. If you are selling at a craft market (see chapter 5), the net income from sales can be relatively high. Sales from your own studio can also be more profitable than selling to stores. If you have your own separate retail outlet, you will have retail selling expenses, but you may still make more profit per sale than you would on sales to shops.

A big advantage when you sell your work directly to the public is that you are paid in cash in most instances. This advantage is hard to beat.

3. Which is best for you?

The type of product you make and the quantities you produce will be the most important factors in determining whether you sell the bulk of your work to shops or directly to the public. If you are producing unique, one-of-a-kind items, it may be possible to sell all your work directly to customers, either through markets, from your own studio or through the mail. If you are making production crafts on a part-time basis, it may also be possible to dispose of your entire output at retail. But if you are making production crafts full-time and have a substantial output, the most effective marketing method is selling to shops. (This, of course, does not rule out selling as much of your work as possible at craft markets or from your own studio.)

Most craftworkers use a variety of marketing channels to sell their work. Chapters 5 and 6 look at each in detail and show you how to sell your work at retail and the best way to get your work into shops.

Before you put your goods on the market, you must first be sure that they are priced to sell and will give you a good profit.

b. PRICING YOUR WORK

Pricing is very important. If your products are priced too low, you will undercut the market and end up working for nothing. On the other hand, if you put too high a price on your work, you will find your goods priced out of the market.

Set a wholesale price for your work first. If you are also selling your work at retail, simply add on an appropriate retail markup. (We'll discuss this in detail in the next chapter.) If you are selling the bulk of your work to shops, bear in mind that most shops will compute the selling price to the customer by doubling your wholesale price.

There are two basic ways you can go about setting wholesale prices for your work.

(a) Cost of production: Using this method you determine all the direct and indirect costs of producing a piece. You add a certain amount over and above this as your profit and you have your wholesale selling price.

(b) Charging what the market will bear: Using this method you look at what similar products are selling for in the marketplace and try to set your prices so that they are not too far above or below those of the main competition.

In practice you will usually find that a combination of both methods works best. Start out by calculating all your production costs or the costs of all your material and labor. Material costs should be fairly easy to calculate. Don't forget to allow a certain amount for waste and remember to include all the materials you use.

Labor costs are a bit more difficult to determine, especially in the beginning stages of your career. Minimum wage rates or prevailing wage rates in your area are of little use to you when you are working for yourself. More important is the time it takes you to produce a piece in relation to the time taken by an experienced craftworker. You certainly can't charge more for a piece simply because it takes you longer to produce it! On the other hand, you do not necessarily have to lower your prices as you become more efficient. As you gain experience, you will earn more per hour from your work.

After calculating your labor and material costs, you then determine your indirect or overhead costs and add a portion of these to the cost of each item you produce. You start by estimating your total overhead costs for a given period of time — usually a year. Be careful not to overlook anything. Think of heat, light, rent, telephone, office supplies, postage, etc. In addition to all these include the time you spend managing the business, designing products, purchasing supplies, selling, etc. All these are very real business costs and if you do not factor them into your selling price, you will be that much out of pocket.

When you have an estimate of your total yearly overhead costs, divide this figure by 12 to arrive at an estimate of your monthly overhead. Estimate as accurately as you can how many of each item you make per month and divide your monthly overhead figure by this amount. The result will be the amount that should be added to the cost of production of each item to cover your overhead.

Now you can add on your net profit figure. This will be the amount you want to clear on each item after you have paid for all the costs of production and overhead costs. You do not need to make the same percentage profit on each item. On some of your bigger, more expensive items you may not want as high a percentage markup as on some of the smaller items. On the average you should aim for a net profit in the range of 15% to 25%. Sample #1 shows a pricing worksheet for Dandy Dolls.

Check your cost of production calculations against the prices of similar work in shops. If your prices appear too high, you must go back to your cost of production figures and recalculate your profit percentages, reduce your hourly labor costs, or try to cut the costs of your raw materials, perhaps by bulk buying (see chapter 9). Alternatively, you may want to avoid selling to shops and instead concentrate your efforts on selling your work directly to the consumer.

The next two chapters look at the best ways to sell your work, both retail and wholesale.

SAMPLE #1
PRICING WORKSHEET

Material costs

Fabric	$1.40	
Filling	.25	
Eyes	.12	
Felt accessories	.28	
Total material costs		$2.05

Labor costs

Sewing	$1.05	
Filling	.15	
Closing	.25	
Finishing	.50	
Total labor costs		$1.95
Total production costs		$4.00

Total overhead per month	$600.00	
Number of units produced per month	800	
Per unit overhead cost		.75
Total per unit cost		4.75
Net profit margin 20%		1.19*
Wholesale selling price		$5.94
Retail selling price		$11.88

---

*To calculate a 20% profit margin, proceed as follows:

80% of the wholesale selling price = $4.75 (i.e., your total cost per unit)
100% of the wholesale selling price = $4.75 ÷ 80 x 100 = $5.94
Profit margin = $5.94 - $4.75 = $1.19

5

RETAILING YOUR WORK

a. RETAILING FROM YOUR STUDIO

If you retail your own products, you are entitled to include the retailer's markup in your selling price. In actual practice, however, most craftworkers will not charge the full retailer's markup on sales of their own work. If you are selling directly to the public from your own workshop, your retail overhead costs should be relatively low. You may be better off by marking up less than the usual 100% retail markup. You will make a little less on each sale, but because of your reasonable prices you will sell more of your work and end up making more money.

However, if you are also selling to shops in the same general area as your studio, it may not be wise to sell your work for substantially less than they do. Some store owners will refuse to handle your work if you are undercutting them on the price. If you do not sell to any local stores, then you won't have this problem, and you can set your retail prices without reference to shops.

Your work will still have to be price competitive with similar work being sold in shops. When you start out, it's a good idea to price your work somewhere in between the highest and the lowest prices charged for similar or competing work. If you sell everything very quickly, you should raise your prices gradually, though not so high that they hamper sales. If your initial prices don't attract a sufficient number of buyers, you will have to lower them.

Location is the single most important factor in retailing. If your workshop is located in a busy shopping area — for example, a main downtown thoroughfare or on a major tourist route — you may be able to sell a large part of your output right out of your own front door. If you happen to be in a very good location for retailing, you might want to set aside a separate retail area in your workshop. You may even want to carry other non-competing crafts as well as your own work. Having different types of work can enhance the attractiveness of your shop and boost sales of your own work.

If you are not in a good location for retailing or if your studio layout or working hours do not lend themselves to retailing, you may be able to sell only a small proportion of your work from your own premises. Rather than trying to attract buyers to you, you may want to take your work to where the buyers are. A good way to do this is to sell your products in a craft market.

b. RETAILING YOUR WORK AT CRAFT MARKETS

Craft markets have provided the launching pad for many successful craft businesses. Unfortunately, not all areas of the country are equally well served by markets, though the number is growing every year. Some metropolitan areas have large, well-organized and well-attended craft markets several times a year.

16

Many rural areas have good craft markets, too. These are frequently connected with community events such as spring festivals, harvest celebrations or county fairs.

Many state and provincial crafts organizations run craft markets. Membership in the organization is usually necessary for participation in the markets. In some cases, the craft markets have a jurying system for entry. Some crafts organizations can provide you with sales leads, or they may have exchanges with their counterparts in other areas so craftworkers can attend markets in other parts of the country. For a list of hundreds of craft markets in the U.S. and Canada, see *The National Directory of Shops/Galleries, Shows/Fairs,* published by Writer's Digest Books. You can write to Writer's Digest at:

> 9933 Alliance Road
> Cincinnati, Ohio 45202

When you enter a craft market, spend some time beforehand planning the layout of your booth and the arrangement of your work. You should create as attractive a selling environment as possible. Make sure you know the booth size in advance so that you can plan your backdrop, tables, and display units and know how much extra stock you can fit into the booth with you. Bring plenty of extra stock. You can't sell from a half empty booth.

You have a good product to sell, so back it up with good sales techniques. Make buying your products as easy as possible for the customer.

(a) Mark prices clearly on everything for sale.

(b) Make sure you have adequate lighting; if at all possible get access to an electrical outlet and arrange your own spot or flood lighting.

(c) Keep a plentiful supply of wrapping paper or bags on hand.

(d) Have your business cards or brochures available for people to take.

Be polite and attentive to your customers, and don't read or talk to your neighbor in the next booth while there are customers around. On the other hand, don't hover over customers and make them feel uncomfortable. Try to look confident and relaxed and *never* appear too anxious to make a sale. Customers appreciate cheerful, attentive service, but most will be turned off if you try a hard sell technique. If possible, engage a customer in casual conversation; it's surprisingly easy to do and sometimes leads to very interesting discussions. But don't get carried away in protracted conversations; remember your purpose is to sell your products.

Craft markets can give your business a tremendous boost. Your net income from sales is relatively high, you are paid in cash, and you meet your customers face to face. These are big advantages, even if the bulk of your sales is to shops.

Craft markets also provide an excellent opportunity to market test your products before you sell them to shops. You can talk to customers about your work or listen to customers' remarks to one another. This can tell you a lot about the attractiveness of your designs, customer appreciation of the quality of your work, and the competitiveness of your prices. In our business, we never sell anything to a shop that we haven't first tried out at a craft market.

If you like travel, you can attend markets in other areas of the country. As more and more markets are organized, you will become increasingly selective.

There are three main criteria you should consider in deciding whether to exhibit at a market:

(a) The quality of the other work being shown. You don't want to damage your reputation by association with low quality shows, bazaars, or flea markets.

(b) How well the market is promoted, i.e., how much advertising is done by the organizers. You don't want to waste your time and money attending a market where there is no advance publicity. In the best craft markets a good proportion of the booth fees goes toward advertising: posters, radio, television, newspaper.

(c) Where is the market located? No matter how much advertising is done, large numbers of buyers won't be attracted unless the location is easily accessible and adequate parking is available.

c. RETAILING YOUR WORK THROUGH THE MAIL

For some craftworkers, mail order has been a profitable way of selling their work. Essentially it works something like this. You write an advertisement for your products and place it in an appropriate medium, such as a weekly newspaper or magazine. Customers see your ad and order your work directly from you through the mails.

Before you actually pay for advertising, however, you should first get as much free advertising as possible. You can get free advertising by using news releases and information pieces that you write yourself and get printed free in trade papers and newspapers. In writing the news release, be as accurate, clear, and brief as possible. Make certain that the following information appears in it: the main selling feature of your work (for example, original wood carvings, winner of the _____ award); the price or range of prices (for example, from $5 to $50); how to order the product and/or a catalogue, if available. (See Sample #2.)

SAMPLE #2
NEWS RELEASE

ROCKINGHORSE CRAFTS LIMITED has just introduced "Pillow Pals," a new line of handcrafted cushions to add to its Doctor Beaver's Friends furry toy animals. The new line features a cat, lamb, elephant, and lion; and more designs are on the way. The cushions are made from the same high quality plush that the Rockinghorse people use in their toys and hand puppets. Filled with polyurethane foam chips, these cute furry creatures have two uses. They can double as playmates for your favorite youngster or as a lovely addition to the room of that very special child. Prices range from $6 to $12 retail. You can order "Pillow Pals" by writing to Rockinghorse Crafts Limited, (*complete address*).

In addition to the news release, you can get free advertising by writing a short article on crafts for the local newspaper or offering yourself for an interview on a local afternoon radio show. This is actually much easier than you might think. Remember, that to most people busy with shopping, housework or office jobs, what you are doing is something quite different from the ordinary and bound to arouse interest.

If your free advertising starts to bring in sales and if you can afford it, you may want to buy a small advertising space in a weekly newspaper or magazine. Since you are now going to pay for advertising, and it is expensive, you want to be certain that your ad is targeted toward the particular market you have in mind. If, for example, your work is selling well in your own home town but you haven't done any business in the prosperous town of Boomsville, 30 miles away, you might consider placing an ad in the *Boomsville Banner*. If it is within your budget, your ad should include a photo or line drawing of one or more of your products. (See Sample #3.)

SAMPLE #3
ADVERTISEMENT

KIDS
LOVE
Rockinghorse
Crafts
TOYS

Send me your FREE full-color catalogue.

Name _____
Street _____
City _____
State/Province _____
Code _____

Tantallon, N.S., Canada B0J 3J0

19

6

WHOLESALING YOUR WORK

a. WHAT KINDS OF SHOPS CAN YOU SELL TO?

Selling your work to stores is probably one of the most effective marketing methods for the full-time production craftworker. By selling your work to stores you can greatly increase the size of your market. Letting stores handle sales to the consumer allows you to concentrate your own time and energy on production and design.

You must be careful to select the best retail outlets for your work. It will help here if we divide possible retail craft outlets into six categories. While not every shop will fall neatly into one of these categories, you will find the classification helpful in deciding where to direct your marketing efforts.

1. The gallery store

A gallery will usually be interested in one-of-a-kind pieces rather than production crafts. Selling your work through a gallery can bring lots of prestige, but in most cases it won't bring you much money on a regular basis unless you have an established reputation in your medium. Galleries are usually interested in work where the value and profit margin are relatively high. A gallery's commission can range up to 50% of the selling price. Moreover, most galleries only accept work on a consignment basis, paying you if and when your work is sold.

2. The craft shop

This type of shop specializes in the sale of high quality handmade work. It is the best outlet for the production craftworker. Consider only craft shops that are in high volume traffic locations and that carry work compatible with your own. Look for stores that carry only high quality work; avoid those that sell cheap "craftsy" items and mass-produced novelties.

There are a few large retail craft enterprises with several branches, but most craft stores are small owner-managed operations, usually run by people with previous experience in the craft field. Some shops are run by craftspeople as an adjunct to their workshop.

There are craft shops that specialize in a particular medium (e.g., wool, pottery). Others are restricted to work of a specific region (e.g., a particular state or province) or a particular theme (e.g., early pioneer). But most shops carry a fairly broad cross section of handcrafted work. (For a list of hundreds of craft shops in the U.S. and Canada, see *The National Directory of Shops/Galleries, Shows/Fairs*, published by Writer's Digest Books.)

3. The gift-craft shop

A gift-craft shop does not usually advertise itself as such, but it is essentially a gift shop that specializes in exclusive, high quality, mass-produced giftware as well as handcrafted products. Giftware covers such a broad range of products that it is almost impossible to define. What is important in looking at the gift-craft shop is the overall quality of the merchandise sold and the reputation of the shop, as well as its location.

Some gift-craft shops have been in business for generations and their names are synonymous with high quality goods. Many of these products are handcrafted though their main selling point is not so much that they are handmade as the fact that their brands or trade names are highly respected and sought after for quality or uniqueness (for example, certain types of English and European porcelain).

For the large scale production craft business the gift-craft shop will be an important outlet. It can frequently sell a higher volume of merchandise than the craft shop. If they carry well-known and popular lines of giftware, gift-craft shops will often be able to afford the big overhead costs associated with locations in very high traffic areas like airports, train stations, and big downtown shopping malls. (Note: shops in places like airports and train stations will sometimes mark up your products by as much as 150%.)

A number of large, high quality gift chains fit into the gift-craft category. These can offer you a regional or even national market. Although their purchasing is not always centralized, a product that is successful in one store has an excellent chance of being sold in other stores in the chain.

For years a friend of mine had been trying to interest one of the major chains in his leather work. Though his work was selling well in craft shops, the chain's head buyer remained unconvinced. One of the chain's stores happened to be located not far from his studio. By dint of sheer persistence and some free samples, my friend persuaded the local store manager to try a small order of his products. They sold very quickly and within a few weeks he got a call from the chain's head buyer. Within a year, my friend's work was being sold by more than a dozen stores in the chain.

A major factor in dealing with a chain is your ability to supply products in the desired quantities, of consistent quality, and on time. These requirements are important in the service you provide to all your customers. The difference in dealing with a chain is that they are likely to require much larger quantities. You must be certain that you can produce the required quantities before you take large orders from a chain. It takes time to increase your output. (See chapters 15 and 16 on expanding your business.)

4. The gift shop

Many of the shops that advertise themselves as gift shops are characterized chiefly by the great variety of low quality, cheap, mass-produced products they sell. These shops are not usually good outlets for handcrafted items.

Occasionally, a gift shop will have a separate section displaying handmade products. Such a shop might be worth considering as an outlet for your work if there is a high volume of business in the area (for example, if the area is a major tourist attraction) and no better quality shop to which you can sell. You must think of your professional reputation. If your work appears in a cheap or junky shop, it may be harder to sell to some of the better quality gift-craft and craft shops.

5. The department store

In the mid-seventies, a few New York stores, such as Saks Fifth Avenue, began selling craft items in a limited way. Now department stores throughout the U.S. and Canada are handling handcrafted items. Some have specialized craft departments, but handcrafted items can be found in a variety of other departments, including gift, jewelry, and housewares.

Department store sales should be considered in the light of their possible effects on your other customers. If you get a large department store order, it may pre-empt an entire season's production. Great, you don't need to worry about finding other customers. But what if the next time around you do not get the large department store order?

Some of your smaller customers may be reluctant to do business with you if you are selling to a large department store in the same area. It is safer not to put all your eggs in one basket. While it's nice to have some large accounts, it's not healthy if any single one of them has too high a proportion of your total sales. If more than 15% or 20% of your business is with a single account, you are probably relying too much on that one customer. Your overall sales and profit situation could be seriously harmed if you fail to secure a big repeat order.

6. Other stores

Outlets for crafts aren't restricted to the above five types. We have sold our toys to a men's dress shop (as props), museum gift shops, and even banks. The list of possible outlets for crafts includes plant, furniture, dress, and sewing shops. Indeed, with a little imagination, you can sell your products to just about any kind of shop where quality merchandise is sold. The first five categories are the most promising places to start. But don't limit yourself to any particular type of shop.

b. HOW TO GET YOUR PRODUCTS INTO SHOPS

1. Calling on stores

At an early stage in your business career, visit those stores in your own area that would appear to be good outlets for your work. Where you start depends largely on the kind of product you have. For one-of-a-kind items, try galleries and craft shops. For production crafts, you might try any of the different types listed above, bearing in mind that the craft shop and the gift-craft shop are probably the best places to start.

When you call on stores, make certain that you talk to the person with purchasing authority. In most cases, this will be the store owner or manager. With chains or department store buyers, an appointment in advance is mandatory. Indeed, it's a good idea to arrange an appointment with any store buyer. Most of these people are extremely busy and your chances of success are much higher if you approach them when they are free to listen to you.

When you meet a store buyer, be as relaxed as possible and confident about your work. When you make your sales pitch, don't be inhibited about praising your own work. If you have a lot of faith in your product, let the buyer know it. You should bring actual samples of your work; don't rely on brochures or photographs. If you have already established a clientele for your work through craft markets or your own retail store, point this out to the buyer. Listen attentively to what the buyer has to say about your product and be prepared to answer any questions.

If you don't get an answer one way or the other during the first visit, be sure to leave a brochure, price list, and business card to remind them of your call. If the store does most of its purchasing during a certain period of the year, be sure to call or visit again at that time.

Once you are successful in placing your products in stores in your immediate area, you may want to extend your marketing efforts further afield. If you enjoy travel and like meeting people, you might want to make extended sales trips to promote your products. Chances are, however, that the demands of production will make it impossible for you to be on the road for long periods if your business is growing. You will need some other way to reach those out of town customers. One way of doing this is to exhibit your products at a wholesale trade show.

2. The trade show

Unlike retail shows, the wholesale, or trade, show is not open to the public but only to store owners who place orders for future delivery. There are only a handful of wholesale craft shows in North America, but there are many regional gift shows. Some of these have separate sections for handcrafted products; most of them are attended by large numbers of buyers in all the major store categories mentioned above.

A wholesale show usually involves more planning than a retail show. But unlike the retail show you do not need to bring a lot of stock with you. Booth fees are usually much higher than for retail shows. In the case of out of town shows, there are travel and accommodation costs as well.

You should draw up a budget for a wholesale show. Make a list of all the expenses you expect to incur and arrive at an estimate of your total costs. Estimate as realistically as possible how much business you expect the show to generate. This can be difficult the first time around, but you should at least know the amount of sales you have to achieve in order to cover your costs. In estimating your costs, don't forget to include your own time while actually selling at the show.

Before exhibiting at a show, it is a good idea to visit the show first as a spectator and do a reconnaissance. Most trade shows are closed to the general public, but you can gain admission as a buyer simply by using your business card or company letterhead. There is a wealth of information to be gained by visiting a show beforehand, looking at the kinds of products for sale, and comparing prices and quality with your own. If you visit a show as a spectator, remember that most of the people there are intent on doing business. Be discreet and don't get in the way.

Plan your booth so that it looks full without appearing overcrowded. Choose the type of display unit that complements your products. Some of the most beautiful displays I have seen were designed and built by craftworkers especially for their own products.

There are display companies and professional booth decorators who will set up your booth for you and provide fixtures, lighting, and carpets, but they are usually very expensive. If you rent a complete booth setup, you are, of course, free of the bother of shipping booth fixtures back and forth. On the other hand, most display companies have a limited variety of fixtures available and what you can rent from them may not be the most appropriate for your products.

Good sales techniques at the show can make a big difference. Dress conservatively and neatly. Be alert and attentive and ready to help the customer at all times. Don't appear bored, and don't read a book in the booth. Some customers will want to browse the booth in a leisurely fashion. Others will want you to conduct them around, describing the products as you go and providing them with any necessary information. Try to feel out how much attention the buyer wants and give it to him or her.

If you are doing a show of two or more days duration, it can be very tiring to run the booth on your own. Try to arrange for help in doing the show or at least get someone to come and relieve you at intervals throughout the day. It is hard to be at your best without a break. Remember, no matter how you feel, you have to be cheerful, confident, and attentive. Learn to distinguish between the lookers and the buyers at a show. Be polite to lookers, but don't waste too much time on them. Concentrate on the buyers.

When you get that order, don't forget to have it signed and get the purchase order number if there is one. Don't be embarassed to ask for the buyer's signature. It is standard business practice. Have your terms of sale, delivery time, and minimum order printed clearly on the order form. If you are selling to someone for the first time, make certain that you check out their credit worthiness before shipping goods to them on credit. When you take the order, ask for credit references. (See the section on granting credit in chapter 14.)

3. The sales representative

Another way to reach out of town customers is to use the services of a sales representative or sales agent. This is someone who will take your samples and literature around to shops and obtain orders for you. He or she is usually paid on a commission basis (a certain percentage of the value of the orders taken).

A good sales representative, or rep, is one of the best ways of reaching new out of town customers and following up on those accounts that you opened at the trade show. Picking the right rep is not easy. In fact, the selection of a sales rep is one of the most difficult problems the small craft business faces. Many craft businesses have had unfortunate experiences with sales reps, frequently because they were not sufficiently selective in their choice.

What should you look for in a rep? You want someone who has an understanding and appreciation of handcrafted work and experience in selling to craft and gift-craft shops. There are very few reps who restrict themselves entirely to handcrafted products; most carry gift lines as well. This in itself should be no problem provided the giftware lines are compatible with your products in quality and price.

One of the most important things to know about a rep is the number and kind of lines he or she is carrying. It does no good to engage a rep who is carrying 30 or 40 other lines. There is simply no way your product can get the attention it deserves from a rep who has so many different products. Find out what size territory the rep is covering. If it's too big, the rep won't be able to properly cover it. Too small a territory, on the other hand, raises the danger that the rep will work it too intensively for a handcrafted product like yours. (See the following chapter on marketing tips for the dangers of overselling your work.)

How do you go about locating a rep? If you have already started to market your work, you may be approached by salespeople who have seen some of your things in stores and craft markets and are interested in representing you. Perhaps a fellow craftworker can recommend a rep. An ad placed in the classified section of the newspaper can sometimes help, though these tend to attract unlikely prospects, such as people with no sales experience. It is better to place your ad in a trade publication where it is more likely to be seen by experienced salespeople. Some trade shows have a notice board where you can put an advertisement for a sales representative.

It is advisable to engage the services of a sales representative for a trial period of, say, six months. This should be long enough in most cases to reveal the kind of results you can expect to get from this rep. A good rep should be able to get your work into stores where he or she has already established connections and is selling other lines. If the rep can't do this much, you have probably picked the wrong person.

Most sales representatives will expect exclusivity within the territory assigned to them. This means that the salesperson is entitled to a commission on all sales within the defined territory. It is usually possible to have a limited number of house accounts, which you have opened yourself and on which you do not have to pay the salesperson any commission. Otherwise, he or she has the territory tied up for the duration of the sales agreement. This is a powerful reason for keeping your initial trial period as short as possible.

Rates of commission for people in the gift/craft business vary, but you can expect to pay anywhere from 10% to 20%, with 15% about the norm. You would pay less to a rep in a territory that you had already substantially opened up, and you would probably have to pay more to a sales agency with a showroom in a major urban location and a force of salespeople on the road.

It is a good idea to offer your rep some kind of incentive plan where the rate of commission escalates on sales over a certain level. Make sure that you have a clear understanding with the rep about when sales commissions are payable. If your customer terms are net 30 days, you will have to wait at least a month for your money. You should pay your salespeople commissions for the month's sales at the end of the following month. You must also retain control over the granting of credit and ship only those orders that meet your credit requirements.

When you sell your work through a sales rep, you must above all be sure that the person who represents you appreciates and believes in your work. Someone who is half-hearted about your products cannot sell them properly. Your sales representative should have some general knowledge of your production techniques so that he or she can explain your work to customers. Your rep should also know your production capabilities, and you should have a mutual understanding about how much business you expect his or her efforts to generate.

4. The wholesale distributor

Many products are sold through wholesalers or distributors who purchase relatively large quantities of goods outright and sell them to retailers in a given territory. An arrangement of this kind can rid you of all marketing problems and enable you to concentrate entirely on production. You are also free of much of the paperwork associated with invoicing, billing, and accounts receivable.

There are, however, very few established distributors or wholesalers of handcrafted products in the U.S. and Canada. One of the main reasons is that most handcrafted products are not able to bear the usual wholesaler markup. This markup can be from 25% to 50% and more, with the retailer's markup on top of that.

A distributor's markup of, say, 40% would mean that an item you sold to the distributor for $10 would be sold by the distributor to the retailer for $14. Since most retailers mark up by 100%, the item would retail for $28 in the store. With sales tax added on (in many jurisdictions), the final price to the customer is likely to be $30 — three times the price you get for the item! Needless to say, there are not many handcrafted items that can sell very briskly when they are marked up this much.

See chapter 17 for information on licensing your product.

7

MARKETING TIPS

a. START OUT CLOSE TO HOME

Tackle the easiest market first. Bear in mind at all times the cost of shipping your goods to market, getting sales, and maintaining contact with your customers. Generally, you will start out in your own town or city and gradually expand sales to other parts of your state or province. There may be a booming market for hand-dipped candles on the East Coast, but if you are a candlemaker on the West Coast, it's better to establish yourself at home first before you try shipping your work across the continent. This doesn't mean that you should turn down an opportunity to sell your work just because the customer is in a distant part of the country. A friend of mine doing handmade clothing in New England got her first big wholesale order from a shop in Anchorage, Alaska.

b. FIND YOUR OWN NICHE IN THE MARKET

Try to find a niche of your own in the marketplace. The possibilities in the craft world are so diverse that it is possible to develop your own particular products. If you are a potter, you may become known for a certain kind of miniature; if you work in leather, you may specialize in painting on your work; if you make sweaters, you may use unique designs.

With experience you will learn just how long you can keep a good selling item on the market. Don't take a good seller out of production just because it has been around for a while. But don't get into a rut and flog a product in the market after it has passed its peak. Keep your line fresh by introducing new products regularly. Be prepared to follow shifts in consumer tastes and demands.

c. AIM FOR THE HIGHEST QUALITY

Exhibit and offer for sale only your best work. Don't try to sell any of your seconds, i.e., work that is flawed in any way, until you have an established reputation for quality work. One of the privileges of being established is that your seconds will find a market. But sell them only as seconds, at a reduced price and in an appropriate marketplace. If you are selling at a craft market, check with the organizers to see if they have any objections to the sale of seconds.

d. AVOID SATURATING THE MARKET WITH A PRODUCT

Most craft products sell best in a given market area when the quantities available in that market are well below the saturation point. This is the point at which the product begins to lose its appeal because there appears to be too much of it on the market. This situation applies to most handcrafted products because of their unique nature. They are different from other commodities because of their aesthetic appeal and because the consumer places a special value on handmade goods.

This puts limits on the size of the market for most handcrafted products in any given geographical area. However, in most cases this saturation point is well beyond the production limits of the individual craftworker, so it is not really a constraint on sales. In other words, unless the market area is very small or very thinly populated, or there are many competitors producing the same product, most craftworkers can sell virtually all they are capable of producing. Moreover, it is usually possible to increase the market for a handcrafted product by expanding sales over a wider area or into a more densely populated area, e.g., a major metropolitan area.

If you have a really hot product with a high saturation point, you may want to expand your business by hiring people to work for you. If you are capable of producing a large quantity of the product, avoid overselling it in any given market area. For instance, George and Susan had a successful stained glass business, selling their work to a variety of good quality craft and gift shops in the New England area. In just a few years, they had built up their business to the point where they employed half a dozen full-time workers and a number of part-time ones. Although they made a variety of different stained glass products, their lampshades were the most popular and accounted for a large part of their business.

George, who was very ambitious, wanted to expand into some of the major gift and department stores. He hired several additional workers and went after some large accounts. He was successful in getting initial orders for lampshades from a number of department stores, including one with a mail order catalogue operation.

At first George and Susan were elated. Then something happened that neither had foreseen. Some of their smaller accounts stopped ordering, because they didn't want to handle products that were being sold by big department stores in their neighborhood. Soon, other stores dropped away too. Some were leery of selling products that were available from a major mail order company, and others claimed that demand for the lampshades had fallen off.

George and Susan became increasingly dependent on relatively few large customers. Within two years, they were forced to cut back drastically and to lay off most of their workers when several of their biggest customers failed to repeat their orders.

George and Susan had oversold their work. Their lampshades were original and appealing. But the appeal was to the kind of customer who wanted something different, the discriminating buyer who sought a product that was not available everywhere. Once the product even *appeared* to be everywhere, it lost much of its appeal.

There are a number of ways that George and Susan could have overcome their problems. If they had diversified and sold a different brand of lampshade to the big stores, they may have been able to keep their small customers as well. Alternatively, they could have introduced new items into the bigger stores under a different name and kept their regular line moving in the smaller gift and craft shops.

e. MAINTAIN GOOD CUSTOMER RELATIONS

Be loyal to your existing customers. You appreciate their loyalty to you, so remember to return their trust. If you have a good account in a particular area, don't open another where it is in direct competition with the first. Say you are selling $2,000 worth of products every summer to the ABC Store in the resort town of Bubbling Brook. If you open up another account in the town, you may find that you still have just $2,000 worth of business in Bubbling Brook, but now it is divided between the ABC Store and your new account.

Service your accounts well. Even if you have a sales representative who makes regular calls, it is a good idea to keep your customers posted about developments in your business. When you introduce new products, send out a photograph or brochure. If you have to increase your prices, give your customers plenty of advance notice and an explanation as to why the increase is necessary. Be prompt to replace any items short-shipped or defective.

f. INCREASING YOUR SALES

If a shop is a good account, stick with it. Try to increase your sales in that particular area by increasing your sales to the existing good account rather than opening another account. Of course, this is not always possible. You may have perfectly good accounts that will buy a certain amount of your work and no more. These stores may feature other kinds of work than yours and may not want to shift their emphasis too much toward your work.

When you sell to craft shops, try to get your work featured if possible. Many craft shops have a relatively small number of items that account for a sizable proportion of their sales. These are the items that are displayed in their front windows and in the most prominent places inside the shop and are featured in their advertisements.

Sales of your work in a particular shop can depend on how your products are displayed and promoted by the shop. Once your products are seen to be good sellers, store owners will naturally give them increased prominence. In the beginning, you have to rely on the appeal of your products to the store owner and your own persuasiveness to get your work prominently displayed.

If a shop is obliged to order a certain minimum quantity of your products each time, this helps ensure that more of your work is displayed. A minimum order policy is also helpful in keeping your paperwork costs down. It may not be possible or wise to require a minimum order when you are starting out. Store owners who are not familiar with your work may be unwilling to buy any more than one or two pieces to test the market. But as soon as you find that your work is selling, you should insist on a minimum order.

It's not uncommon for a shop to want to be the exclusive outlet for your product in a given area. There is nothing inherently wrong with an exclusive arrangement, provided that the shop is able to realize the potential for sales of your products in that area. When you are starting out, it is difficult to know potential sales, so be careful with any exclusive arrangement and keep it initially to a relatively short period of time.

g. REPEATS TELL THE TALE

Repeat orders are the measure of your success in the marketplace. Placing the initial order in a shop is just the beginning. What you want is an active repeat business. Once you are established a large part of your business will be repeats.

h. SET REALISTIC MARKETING GOALS

Be patient. Rome wasn't built in a day. You have to work hard to build up a clientele. Set realistic marketing goals. Remember, it took time to perfect your production techniques; it takes time to work out a successful marketing system. The thing to be concerned about at any given point in the development of your business is not so much the actual volume of your sales but the trend of sales and whether or not it is steadily increasing.

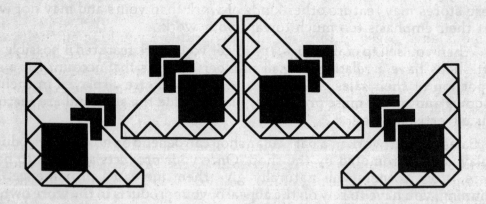

8

YOUR WORKSHOP

a. WHERE TO LOCATE YOUR WORKSHOP

Let's assume that you have passed the initial start-up phase of your business. You have learned how to make a line of marketable products, you have successfully put your products into stores, and repeat orders are coming in. At this point you will want to give more thought to the production side of your business, starting perhaps with your workshop.

Perhaps you were fortunate enough to have had an adequate workshop from the beginning and you do not need to create any additional space at this stage. But sooner or later you will find that your growing business requires extra space or at least a reorganization of your existing space. In some cases, say, in a basement workshop, it may be possible to have a larger working space simply by knocking out a partition or two and making the room bigger. Or perhaps you can expand your operation to the garage as well as the basement. Some craftspeople have even built on additions to their homes to accommodate their craft businesses.

Renting outside space is another option you might want to consider. If you live in a one bedroom apartment, it may be impossible to expropriate enough space for your business and you will have to consider buying or renting outside accommodation. There may be a nearby barn or garage that can be converted into a workshop. If you are in a city, you might find an elderly but still sturdy building in the downtown area. If you plan to make changes to rented premises, be sure to have an agreement with the landlord regarding leasehold improvements.

If at all possible, you should try to operate out of your home, as there are enormous advantages to this. By working at home you save all the time and expense of traveling back and forth between home and workplace. You can avoid making large capital outlays or paying rent for workspace and thereby increase the profits of your business. You can claim a portion of your home expenses, heat, light, and telephone as a tax deduction. You can also more easily employ other members of your family in your business if you want.

If your workshop is located in your home, you will likely be able to operate without any special permission from the local authorities. This is an enormous advantage, especially in the beginning. You don't want bureaucratic hassles while you are trying to establish your business. Most cities and towns have regulations about the kinds of businesses that can be carried out in private residences. Chances are, however, that these will not be too strenuously enforced unless you become a nuisance to a neighbor, in which case the city will have to act. If you are located in the country, interference with neighbors is much less likely to be a problem. (See the section on licenses in chapter 10.)

b. PLANNING A WORKSHOP

When planning a workshop, whether in your own home or in a separate location, make sure that you will have enough space for your immediate requirements and that it is relatively easy to add more space should this become necessary in the future.

If you plan to do a lot of retailing from your workshop, you may have to add parking space, unless there is an abundance of street parking in your area. Zoning regulations may have to be considered. A building approved for use as a workshop may not necessarily conform to local regulations if it is used as a retail outlet.

1. The building

If you are constructing a new building, you have a big advantage in that you can plan the layout to suit your exact requirements. Draw up your plans carefully, thinking of things like the location of doors and windows and electrical requirements. Have as many windows as possible on the south side. Make certain that doorways are big enough to accommodate anything you will likely want to bring in or take out of the building.

If you are putting up a new building, you will need permission from the local authorities. Zoning requirements vary greatly from one area to another. The city (or county, if the business is located in an unincorporated area) can give you information concerning the zoning requirements of the area where you plan to locate. Before beginning construction you must apply for a building permit. This usually requires the submission of preliminary sketches of the building for approval and sometimes, at a larger stage, complete construction drawings.

If you plan to purchase and renovate an existing building, be sure that the use to which you plan to put it will conform to local regulations. If the building formerly housed an established business, it is possible that the business was set up before the local regulations went into effect. It may be that the owner of such a building is exempt from zoning regulations until he or she applies for a building permit to make structural changes or additions to the building. Always check first with the building department before purchasing an existing building for use as a workshop or retail outlet for your crafts.

When building or making major renovations, plan as far ahead as possible for any special requirements you may have. Make certain that there are enough electrical outlets and that they are located where you can use them. Extension cords running all around your workshop are a serious safety hazard and they can get you into trouble with your fire insurance company. Consider also the size and type of electrical service in the building. Is it adequate for the type of equipment you plan to use? If you need three phase electrical service, check first with the power company to be sure that it is available in your area and find out how much extra it costs.

If you put up a new building with its own electrical service, you will probably end up paying commercial rates for electricity, and these are a good deal higher than domestic rates in most areas. If you are operating from your basement or garage and using your home electrical service, there is no reason why you have to pay commercial rates, at least in the beginning.

The same applies to your telephone. There will come a time when you may want a business telephone listing but with most craft businesses this will not be necessary in the beginning. If at all possible, run your electrical equipment from your house and use your home telephone.

When planning your workshop, pay attention to ventilation. Usually an open window is sufficient, but if you are doing certain types of work, such as pottery with an unvented electric kiln, a properly vented electric fan should be installed. If your work creates a lot of dust, for example, sawdust from woodcutting or woodsanding operations, you should install hoods or vents over your equipment and have the dust particles or sawdust exhausted to the outside by an electric fan.

If you plan to locate your workshop in a building housing other tenants, you should ensure that your operations do not interfere with them. You don't want complaints about the noise or smells created by your business. Likewise, you won't want to locate your workshop next to a business that creates a lot of noise or dust or one that has heavy vehicles coming and going at all hours of the day.

What about security? If your workshop is located away from your house, it will be vacant at night and on the weekends. Make sure that doors and windows are lockable and that you carry adequate insurance protection. Your coverage should include not only the building itself but tools, equipment, and stock on the premises.

2. The interior

Plan the interior layout of your workshop with the various operations of your craft in mind. You will work more efficiently and comfortably if you can isolate different parts of the work process in different areas of the workshop. This keeps tools and equipment from getting mixed up and prevents materials from contaminating one another.

When you plan the layout of work benches and tables, think of the flow of work from design to completion. Try to avoid carrying tools and work back and forth any more than necessary. Even in a small one-person operation, a good layout of tools and working areas in the workshop can make a great difference to the efficiency and profitability of your craft business. If you have employees working for you, efficient organization in the workshop is even more important.

Set aside separate areas for the storage of raw materials and finished goods. This helps immensely when taking inventory and handling orders. Allow plenty of space in the various working areas for the temporary storage of work in progress. If you have to store work at certain stages while you wait for the paint to dry or the material to cool off, think about where you're going to put it so it won't be in your way while you carry on with another part of the operation.

What about a separate area for office or showroom space? If you are pressed for space, a combination of office and showroom area at one end of your workshop is a good idea. Both office and showroom requirements are similar — a clean, quiet place away from the hurly-burly of the workbench where you can show your products to visitors and potential buyers or eat your lunch.

If you are planning to do a lot of retailing from the workshop, you may want to set aside a separate area. This need not be partitioned off from the working area. In fact, if you are interested in demonstrating your work, it may actually help sales if people can watch you at work. On the other hand, some craftspeople find this a distraction and prefer to keep the selling and production sides of their craft separate. They may want to have a separate shop, partitioned off from the workshop or even have a retail shop in another location.

To sum up: your workshop should be a pleasant and comfortable place in which to work, whether located in your own home or in a separate building. But remember that buildings don't produce profits. They merely provide the working space for you and your tools and equipment. They are part of the overhead costs of your business, and your overhead should always be kept as low as possible.

If the needs of your business outgrow your workshop, you can expand to more spacious quarters. If your business is growing, this makes good sense. But wait until your business is ready for it before you take on increased overhead costs. Don't expand too soon and incur large fixed costs that could bankrupt you if business falls off.

9
PRODUCTION

As a businessperson, your goal is to cut costs, increase efficiency, and make as much money as possible. This chapter looks at how you can do this.

a. BULK BUYING

Whenever possible, you should buy your raw materials in bulk. There are tremendous savings to be realized by the bulk purchase of most items. Of course, buying in bulk requires the outlay of more capital so it is not recommended until you have got your business off the ground.

As well as buying in bulk, you should try to get as close as possible to the source of your raw materials. In the beginning, you may buy your supplies from a retail craft supply or hobby supply store. In fact, it is not worthwhile trying to "source" all your raw materials at the start of your business. You have other more important things to do at this stage. But as soon as your business is off and running, you will want to get as close as possible to the manufacturer of your raw materials. This is not always easy. Many wholesalers and distributors are unwilling to identify their sources of supply, and sometimes manufacturers will only sell their products through a distributor.

Most wholesalers deal in minimum quantities, which are usually more than the quantities you need or can afford to buy in the beginning. To the average wholesaler, your miniscule order may not be worth the trouble. Getting wholesalers to agree to do business with you is sometimes a feat in itself, requiring all the arts of persuasion that you can muster. It usually helps if (without blatant deception) you can somehow implant in the wholesaler's mind the vague notion that someday your company may be a tremendous success and will order huge quantities of their products.

It helps also if you agree to pay cash for initial shipments. In most cases, you'll have little choice anyway when you are starting out. Later on when you have reached the point where your orders are more substantial, you can apply for credit. Don't expect to get it in the beginning.

If you know other craftworkers who use the same material, it may be possible to organize cooperative buying. When you have been in business for some time and get to know other craftworkers in your field, you may find several with whom you could work smoothly in such a cooperative.

Your purchasing can be greatly simplified if you design your products with a view to multiple uses of material as much as possible. Besides simplifying purchasing, this helps keep your inventory costs down. If you are ordering material that can be used in only one single item, you will have a problem if sales of that particular item decline. You will be stuck with material that doesn't fit into anything else that you are making.

b. STORAGE

Buying relatively large quantities of raw materials raises the question of storage. This will be more or less of a problem depending on how bulky your raw materials and finished products are. If you are working in jewelry, storage may not be a major concern, but in woodworking and certain other crafts, storage can be a big problem.

It is no good buying your raw materials in bulk if the savings of bulk buying are offset by the costs of storing your materials until you're ready to use them. You can greatly lower your storage costs and take advantage of bulk buying by using dead storage space. This is simply space outside your studio or workshop where you can store materials for relatively long periods of time. In most cases, this kind of storage will be considerably cheaper than workshop space.

c. ORDERS

You need a simple system for keeping track of customer orders to be certain that you ship the right things to the right place at the right time. Without a system, you will have to rely on memory or conduct room to room searches of your house and workshop to find a particular order. Shipping the wrong things or shipping an order late can cost you a lot in money and customer goodwill.

Keep your orders in an order book or file them in file folders according to the requested shipping date. This helps you batch shipments together with a similar shipping date and save time by taking a batch of parcels to the post office or having them picked up. It is much easier to plan your production if you can tell at a glance just how much business you have "on the books." (See Sample #4.)

d. PACKING

How you pack your work for shipment to the customer is very important. Even the most beautiful piece of pottery isn't very impressive in several hundred small pieces. But breakables aren't the only problem. Many articles require special packing to prevent them from being squashed, scratched by rubbing together, wrinkled or otherwise damaged in transit.

If you are shipping relatively few, large or expensive one-of-a-kind pieces, your packing problems are different from those of someone making production items. Each unique piece will require its own individually designed container, which in the case of large, fragile items, should be a sturdy wooden crate, literally built around the piece.

For most production work, you can use corrugated cardboard cartons. These are available in various degrees of thickness, depending on the nature of the products you are shipping. You will probably have to salvage cartons from your friendly neighborhood supermarket or liquor store in the beginning, but as your business grows, you may want to have your own cartons made with your name stamped on the outside. Obviously, it is cheaper if you can use just one single size carton for all of your products.

36

When you pack your products, fill in all the spaces left inside the container so that the piece or pieces in the box cannot move around. Depending on what you are packing, crumpled newspaper, excelsior, plastic bubble wrap or foam rubber will make good packing material. Your cartons should be sealed with strong self-adhesive packing tape, preferably reinforced.

Some carriers have wrapping restrictions. For example, United Parcel Service (UPS) requires that packages be made of corrugated cardboard, with no string or paper on the outside, and sealed with reinforced tape.

e. SHIPPING

Mark any special shipping instructions clearly on the outside of your cartons. Glass and other fragile articles should have a wine glass symbol stenciled on each side of the box. Write the address directly on the carton with a waterproof marker or affix a gummed label. Mark your return address prominently on the outside of the carton.

Where possible follow the customer's instructions as to how goods should be shipped. If this is not possible, ship the cheapest route. In the U.S. and Canada, most points can be reached by parcel post. Check with your local post office for size and weight restrictions. In the U.S., United Parcel Service (UPS) will accept packages up to 50 pounds in weight and 108 inches length and girth combined. Canada has no service comparable to UPS, but Canpar and Canadian Pacific Package Express offer fairly widespread coverage in many provinces.

For fast shipment, there is a growing number of airfreight services in the U.S. and Canada. Many of these promise overnight delivery (though they don't always live up to their promises). They are also fairly expensive and should not be used unless a customer specifically requests it.

Insure all shipments no matter how you ship them. Some services have automatic insurance; UPS, for example, automatically includes insurance up to $100. Where this is insufficient, additional insurance should be purchased. The relatively small extra charge involved is well worth it and can save you a lot of grief if the shipment fails to arrive at its destination.

f. INVENTORY

1. How to keep track of it

It would be ideal if you had firm orders for all of your work. Some craftspeople do, in fact, produce only on commission but most production craftworkers find that they have to keep additional supplies of goods on hand at all times. Customers expect you to supply exactly what they want when they want it.

Your inventory consists of your raw materials and work in progress as well as your finished products. Careful management of your inventory can have a major impact on your cash flow, production schedule, and profits.

You need an inventory control system or a set of records of everything that goes into or comes out of inventory. This will tell you which of your products is moving well, when you need to reorder supplies and when to produce in order to have adequate quantities of goods available for filling orders.

You can keep this information on index cards, in a looseleaf notebook or on a columnar pad. It should show additions to and deletions from each particular item that you are keeping track of and have a column showing the current inventory holding of each item.

Each item in your inventory should have a reorder point. When the quantity is reduced to this reorder point, you produce or reorder that particular item. Experience will soon tell you how fast you use up your materials at a given level of output and how long it takes each of your suppliers to ship materials to you. (See Sample #4.)

2. How big should your inventory be?

How big an inventory of finished goods should you carry? You must know how fast your finished goods move out of the workshop to your customers. As a rough check on the overall size of your inventory, there is a simple calculation that you can do. Compare your total inventory with your average monthly sales. Say, for example, you had the following sales for the last half of the year.

July	5,000 widgets
August	4,500 widgets
September	4,500 widgets
October	6,000 widgets
November	7,500 widgets
December	4,000 widgets

Total sales for the six months = 31,500

Average monthly sales = 5,250

ORDER BOOK AND INVENTORY LIST FOR "PINECRAFT CO."

ITEM	LG. BOWL RP = 40				SM. BOWL RP = 90				MED. BOWL RP = 50				LG. TRAY RP = 40			
DATE	ORDERS	SHIPPED	MADE	BAL. STOCK	ORDERS	SHIPPED	MADE	BAL. STOCK	ORDERS	SHIPPED	MADE	BAL. STOCK	ORDERS	SHIPPED	MADE	BAL. STOCK
JUNE 2	20			50	35		40	90	30		20	29				45
JUNE 3		5		45	20	15		75	20	10	60	79				
JUNE 4	25				40		50	125			35	79	8	8		37
JUNE 5	20	5		40	10	30		95	25	55		59		10		27

RP = REORDER POINT (at this point more of each item would be reordered or made)
ORDERS = All orders on hand for this item
SHIPPED = Number of items shipped — inventory deletions
MADE = Number of items made — inventory additions
BAL. STOCK = Number of items currently in inventory

Your inventory at the end of December is 7,800. Since you have found that a total inventory of about 30 days average sales is sufficient for normal operation and you know that the two months following December are your slack season, you could reduce your inventory to around 5,250 and still have plenty of stock on hand to fill orders.

If you are working with an assistant or one or more employees, you will probably want to reduce your inventory in a case like this in order to keep your costs down. However, if you are running your craft business single-handedly, you may want to allow your inventory to remain a little higher than the above formula would suggest. The reason for this is as follows. You will most likely find that there are fairly pronounced seasonal fluctuations in your sales. The pre-Christmas buying season may be one of your busiest times or the spring months may be your peak sales period. If you are running a single-person operation, you will spend a lot of your time selling, shipping, and invoicing in the peak periods and you will not be able to do as much production. You must therefore build up your inventory in anticipation of these busy sales periods.

3. How much of each item should you carry?

Apart from the overall size of your finished goods inventory, there is the question of just how much of each particular item you should carry. Even if you are making a single product, there are likely to be several different styles and sizes. More likely you will have a variety of different items. How much of each particular item should you carry in inventory?

If you break down your inventory and sales figures as in the diagram below, you may find that one or two items account for a relatively large proportion of your sales.

Products	% inventory	% of sales
A, B	30	70
C, D	30	20
E, F, G	40	10

From this you can see that items A and B should receive the most attention, as they account for 70% of your sales. You can reduce your inventory of items E, F and G, as they are relatively unimportant to your total sales picture.

Even though you are close enough to your business to know which items are your best movers, it is worthwhile to do this little analysis for verification. No matter how small your business, you want to plan your production so that you concentrate your efforts on those products that are selling best.

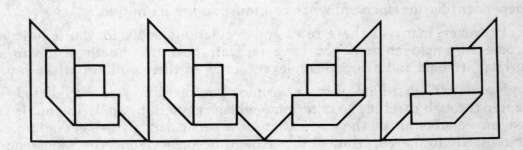

10

RULES AND REGULATIONS

This chapter contains vital information that you as a professional craftsperson or operator of a craft business must know. It is here rather than at the beginning of the book for a very good reason. If you start off by reading this chapter first, you may feel that there are so many complex government rules and regulations that you would be better off *not* going into business.

Government in its wisdom has decreed that as a businessperson you are automatically appointed to the job of an unpaid tax collector (whether you like it or not). Government has also created a vast body of legislation telling you, the independent businessperson, what you must and must not do.

However, many of these rules and regulations apply to you only if you become an employer or if you have separate business premises. If you are working at home and have no employees, most of them will not affect you.

No matter what kind of craft business you operate, you should read this chapter through carefully to determine which regulations apply to you. If you have any doubts about the application of a particular law or regulation, you should write to the government department or agency concerned and request clarification with respect to your situation.

The following sections apply to both the U.S. and Canada. Where there are significant differences between the two countries, as in the case of payroll taxes, they are treated separately.

a. RETAIL SALES TAX

Most U.S. states and Canadian provinces charge a retail sales tax. This tax is levied on all sales directly to the consumer. If you are selling your work directly to the consumer and you are in a jurisdiction that has this tax, you are responsible for collecting it and remitting it to the government at regular intervals. You are required to apply for a sales tax number from the department of revenue or finance. They will issue you a certificate of authority to collect the tax, send you reporting forms and all necessary instructions, and advise you of dates (usually monthly) for remitting tax collected.

If you have a state or provincial retail sales tax permit, you do not have to pay retail sales tax on materials bought for use in products you plan to resell. Some merchants may want you to fill out a form of declaration stating that the goods purchased are intended for use as a component part in an article for resale, but most will be content to have your state or provincial retail sales tax number.

b. FEDERAL SALES TAX (in Canada only)

This is an ideal tax from the government's point of view because it is invisible, at least as far as the majority of voters are concerned. The federal sales tax, currently at 12%, is levied on the sale price of most goods manufactured or produced in Canada. The manufacturer or producer is required to collect this tax from the purchaser (wholesaler or retailer) and remit it to the provincial branch of the sales and excise tax office at monthly intervals. (In certain circumstances, quarterly returns are possible.)

If you are a manufacturer in Canada, you are required to obtain a sales tax license which is issued by the Federal Sales Tax Office. This permits you to purchase or import articles or materials free of federal sales tax when certified to be used in, wrought into or attached to taxable goods for resale.

The federal sales taxes collected must be remitted on a special form which is due on or before the end of the following month. (This can be a real hardship for small businesses with a lot of charge sales, since they won't have received all their money from customers before the end of the following month.)

Fortunately, there is some relief for the small craft business owner. If you have less than $50,000 gross of sales, you are not required to collect federal sales tax. Also, certain types of crafts, such as stained glass and sculpture, are exempt from the federal sales tax. Like most aspects of Canadian tax law, the federal sales tax regulations are enormously complex and frequently revised. If you have any questions about your particular product, write for information:

Revenue Canada — Taxation
Information Services
123 Slater Street
Ottawa, Ontario
K1A 0L8

They will send you complete information as to whether your business is obliged to charge the federal sales taxes.

c. PAYROLL TAXES

If you are an employer in the U.S. or Canada, you have to collect taxes from your employees. For governments, taxation at source is the best thing that was ever invented. For employers, it means that you spend a lot of your time as an unpaid tax collector. Payroll taxes are the main reason why hiring people to work for you will just about double your paperwork.

After reading this section, you may well decide that you *don't* want to become an employer. In this case, turn to the last section in this chapter to discover how you may be able to have work done without becoming an employer.

1. If you are in the United States

To meet your legal obligations as an employer, you should write to the federal and state tax departments at least one month before hiring your first employee.

(a) Federal requirements

Contact the Internal Revenue Service and tell them that you are about to become an employer. They will send you an application for an employer's identification number, an employer's tax guide, which includes a set of federal withholding tables and sample forms, and all the other information that you need.

The amount of income tax that you must withhold from each employee's paycheck is determined by using the withholding tables. You are also obliged to withhold the social security tax or F.I.C.A. (Federal Insurance Contributions Act). This must be matched by an equal amount from you as an employer.

These amounts must be remitted by you on the federal payroll tax return, a special form which you will receive compliments of the IRS. If the amounts collected are less than $500, they may be remitted quarterly; if they exceed $500, other due dates apply depending on the amounts collected. (They may be due as soon as three banking days after the end of the payroll period.) Remittances may be made to an authorized commercial bank or a Federal Reserve bank.

The F.I.C.A. tax is not payable for an individual employed by his or her spouse and/or a child under the age of 21 employed by a parent.

As an employer you are also liable for the federal unemployment tax. This is a tax imposed on you the employer; you do not deduct it from your employee's wages. This tax applies if you paid wages of more than $1,500 in a calendar quarter in the current or preceding calendar year. *Read the instructions about this carefully.* An annual return is filed on a special form which will be sent to you.

(b) State requirements

Most states in the U.S. have an income tax on wages and require employers to withhold state income tax. Most states also have employer paid state unemployment insurance. Contact your state department of employment and request the state employer's tax guide, withholding tables, and instructions.

Many states require employers to have workers' compensation insurance. This provides wage, disability, and death benefits to employees hurt or killed on the job. Some states have their own insurance plans, others require that you obtain coverage with a private insurance company.

2. If you are in Canada

You should write to Revenue Canada at least a month before becoming an employer and request an employer's tax number, tax guide, and tables for the amounts to be withheld from employees' pay. Income tax, Canada Pension Plan contributions, and unemployment insurance premiums must be deducted from each employees' paycheck in accordance with sets of tables which Revenue Canada will send you.

As an employer, you are required to contribute an employer's portion to both the pension plan and unemployment insurance plan. Pension plan deductions from employees must be matched by an equal amount from you the employer. Unemployment deductions must be accompanied by an amount that is (at time of writing) 1.4 times the amount deducted from the employee.

The amounts deducted from employees, together with employer contributions, must be remitted to Revenue Canada, accompanied by a special form which they will send you. Remittances are due on the fifteenth of the following month and may be made at any branch of a chartered bank or by mail.

Workers' compensation is usually provided by a provincial workers' compensation board. If you have employees, you will be assessed on the basis of the size of your payroll according to a rate scale that is based on industry statistics. This admittedly can be unfair to a small craft operation, since most craft businesses don't correspond to standard industry classifications. For example, a small woodworking shop making handcrafted furniture may be assessed on the basis of rates for the furniture industry.

d. DEADLINES FOR GOVERNMENT REMITTANCES

Whether you operate in the U.S. or Canada, you should be aware that deadlines for sales taxes and payroll taxes are rigorously enforced. If a remittance is due on or by the fifteenth of the month, for example, it must be paid on or by the fifteenth. If you are even one day late, you are subject to automatic fines.

Also in both countries you are presumed to know the law. As horrifying as this may seem, ignorance of the law is no proper legal grounds for noncompliance. Whenever you are in doubt about whether a particular statute applies to your business, write to the department or agency concerned and get the full facts.

e. LICENSES

Most towns, municipalities, and counties in the U.S. and Canada require businesses to have a local business license. This can cost anywhere from $10 to $200 and is usually renewed annually. But a license will rarely be necessary if you operate a small craft business out of your home. (See chapter 8 on your workshop.) Discretion and prudence are the key words here. If you are quietly producing handmade widgets in your basement, no one will likely bother you.

But if you expand the retail side of your operation to the point where you have signs prominently displayed and a lot of customers coming and going, you are likely to attract the attention of the local authorities, who may require you to hold a license.

If you have a separate workshop building or retail outlet, you wll be subject to all the licensing requirements, zoning laws, building regulations, health and fire codes that your local government has devised. You will also be subject to local taxes on real estate, water consumption, and business premises. Real estate taxes are based on the assessed real value of your property. Business taxes are usually applied directly against the tenant or business operator. Business taxes may be based on the property assessment, the annual rental value, the value of year-end inventory or on some other basis.

It is impossible to detail the requirements of all local governments. Any or all of the above local taxes and regulations might apply to you. If you have separate business premises, the safest bet is to write your local authority *before* opening your doors for business. Also, wherever possible, operate your business out of your own home, at least in the beginning. Later on, when things are off and running, you may need separate premises, and you can tackle the local bureaucracy then.

f. LABELING

Depending on what you make there are certain labeling requirements you should be aware of.

1. In the U.S.

All packages and labels on goods must conform to the Federal Fair Packaging and Labeling Act. This requires that a label identify the product, give the name of the manufacturer or distributor, and show the net quantity of the contents. You can get a copy of the act from the Federal Trade Commission, Washington, D.C., 20580.

Textiles, fabrics, and clothing must be labeled in accordance with the Textile Fibre Products Identification Act and Federal Trade Commission Act regarding the care labeling of wearing apparel. Essentially, the first of these laws requires that textile, fabric, and clothing labels state the fibre content or composition of the fabric, the name of the manufacturer or distributor, and the country of origin if the goods are imported. The second piece of legislation requires that labels on finished wearing apparel or piece goods intended to be made into wearing apparel "clearly disclose instructions for the care and maintenance of such goods" (e.g., lukewarm wash, etc.). The Federal Trade Commission will supply you with copies of these laws.

A few states, e.g., Maine, require that *upholstered or stuffed articles* have labels identifying the stuffing material.

2. In Canada

In Canada, prepackaged products must have a label identifying the product, the manufacturer or distributor, and showing the net quantity (where applicable). The quantity must be in metric units and the information must be printed in both English and French.

Textiles, fabrics, and wearing apparel must be labeled with the fibre content or composition of the fabric according to the Textiles Labelling Act. There are other regulations governing the sale of consumer textile fabric products. For detailed information, contact:

> Department of Consumer and Corporate Affairs
> Place du Portage
> Hull, Quebec
> K1A 0C9

Some Canadian provinces require the makers of *stuffed articles* to be licensed and to label all products with the type of stuffing used and whether it is new or used material. Fortunately, the provinces that have these requirements will accept the label authorized by the province of Ontario. To apply for an Ontario license, write:

> Government of Ontario
> Ministry of Consumer and Commercial Relations
> Upholstered and Stuffed Articles Branch
> 3300 Bloor Street West, 3rd Floor
> Toronto, Ontario
> M8X 2X4

g. CONTRACTS

If you are engaged in production crafts, selling your work is fairly straightforward, involving simply a sales slip or invoice. It is advisable to get a signed purchase order, particularly for a new account. If the order is a large one, you should insist on a signed purchase order before proceeding with the work. A contract should be signed if goods are ordered to a customer's particular specifications.

If you are producing one-of-a-kind pieces, you will probably use contracts more often than someone in production crafts. If you produce a unique piece of work for a particular customer, it may be unsalable elsewhere and involve a considerable amount of your time and raw materials. To protect yourself, some kind of written contract is mandatory.

In the United States, there are certain situations where the law requires a contract to be in writing. The Statute of Frauds in effect in most states, requires any agreement that cannot be completed within one year to be in writing. If, for example, you are commissioned to produce a wall hanging to be installed in the foyer of a new building to be completed in 18 months, the agreement must be in writing to be legally valid.

If you are making relatively expensive one-of-a-kind pieces in the U.S., you may also be affected by the Uniform Commercial Code. This statute, which is in effect in most states, requires a written contract whenever goods over $500 in value are sold.

A contract can be anything from a simple verbal agreement to a 20-page legal document. Essentially it should cover what is to be produced, the cost, method of payment, and completion date, and it should provide methods for resolving any possible problems that could arise in the course of the transaction.

Here are some of the points that should be covered in a contract.

If you sell a unique piece directly to a client, you should consider a simple written agreement covering the following:

(a) Date of sale, name of purchaser, description of the work, price

(b) Terms of payment; in the case of a work that involves a substantial commitment in time or raw materials, you should structure the contract so that you receive several progress payments. A useful arrangement would be for you to receive a design fee when the agreement is signed, a second progress payment upon completion of a distinct phase of the work, and final payment upon completion of the whole work.

(c) Whether you want to reserve reproduction rights

If you place a work with a shop or gallery on consignment, you should include the following:

(a) The selling price and how it is to be set

(b) The percentage to be paid to you (while this should be in the range of 70 to 75% when dealing with craft shops, some of the more prestigious galleries will demand more — sometimes up to 50% — in the case of unique one-of-a-kind pieces)

(c) Whether the shop or gallery has exclusive rights and, if so, in what area

(d) Whether the shop or gallery receives any commissions on direct sales by the artist/craftsperson

(e) Who is responsible for insurance while the work is on exhibit

(f) The duration of the agreement

h. INCOME TAXES

Laws governing income tax for businesses and individuals are extremely complex. Moreover, they are subject to constant changes and in some cases even to different interpretations. In the chapter on accounting you are advised to seek the advice of a competent professional for your business income taxes.

i. HOW TO AVOID BECOMING AN EMPLOYER

The U.S. Internal Revenue Service and Revenue Canada define an employee in similar terms. According to the IRS: "Everyone who performs services subject to the will and control of an employer both as to what shall be done and how it shall be done, is an employee. It does not matter that the employer permits the employee considerable discretion and freedom of action, if the employer has the legal right to control both the method and the result of the services. Though not always applicable, some of the characteristics of the term 'employee' are that the employer has the right to discharge him and furnishes him with tools and a place to work."

It is possible for certain small businesses, especially craft businesses, to get work done without hiring employees. They do this by hiring outside contractors, that is, people who sell their services for a fee. When you hire an outside contractor, you pay this person his or her full fee. You do not deduct or withhold taxes or social security contributions.

Chapter 16 on hiring explains how to operate a craft business on a "cottage industry" basis. Instead of having employees who come to your workshop, you have products made for you by people who work at home, using their own tools and working their own hours. The pros and cons of this arrangement from the point of view of the economics of production are also discussed later.

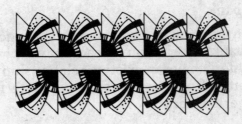

11

GETTING HELP

a. GETTING A BANK LOAN

If you are fortunate, your craft business will be able to generate sufficient cash to meet its operating requirements and you won't need to borrow money. The cost of borrowing is an extra business expense, and the fewer expenses you have the better.

However, many successful craft businesses from time to time need extra cash. It may be that your sales have expanded rapidly and you need an operating loan for a relatively short period of time. Or perhaps you are putting up a new workshop and require longer term financing.

Where you go for financial help depends on whether you are in the U.S. or Canada. The U.S. banking system is much more responsive to the needs of small enterprises than is the banking system in Canada. If your business is in Canada, you are much more likely to go to some government agency for a loan. But this difference aside, loan application procedures are similar in both countries.

1. Select the right bank

The first step is to select the bank or banks that you are going to approach. The best bet is to select a bank where you already have a history of responsible financial dealings. If you don't have an existing relationship with a bank, you may want to shop around a bit to find one that suits you in terms of location or how approachable the manager appears.

2. Be well prepared

Always be well prepared when you approach a banker. You will feel more confident, and the banker is likely to be impressed by your organization if you have a good, typewritten presentation.

Present the banker with a statement of your cash flow (see chapter 14 on preparing a cash flow statement) and explain precisely how much money you want to borrow and why. Be precise and very specific. Show how your business can be expected to generate the cash to repay the loan.

3. Provide past financial data

Be prepared to provide financial statements (profit and loss statements and balance sheets) for the last three years of operation of your business. If you have been in business for a shorter period of time, you should bring all your existing

50

financial statements. If you are borrowing money to get your business started, you won't have past financial records so you should put increased emphasis on the future projections for your business. (See chapter 14 on how to prepare an operating forecast.)

4. Be prepared to sell yourself

When you approach a banker for a loan, you are selling yourself, your ideas, and your ambitions. If you want to win his or her confidence, you must be prepared to answer all the banker's questions as candidly as possible. Bring a personal resume that includes your general and educational background. Provide the banker with details of your personal financial situation: how much personal debt you have and what assets you own.

5. Security for your loan

The question of security for your loan will inevitably arise. You can be sure that your banker will not lend you money unless you have some tangible assets as security. Your strategy should be to sell the banker on your business plans and their soundness before discussing what security you can give. If you own your own home and are willing to mortgage it, or mortgage it further if you are currently making mortgage payments, a banker is likely to lend you money on it.

6. Personal guarantees

When you borrow money for your business, you are personally liable to pay it back. If your company is incorporated, the bank will require a personal guarantee from you. Your bank may also require you to sign an assignment of receivables declaration which gives the bank legal authority to step in and collect any money owed to you by your customers if your business goes under. You may also have to sign a postponement of claim declaration which, in effect, gives the bank priority over all other creditors of your company including yourself in bankruptcy proceedings. Whatever specific requirements your banker may have, you can be sure that they will be rigorous.

If they agree to grant you a loan, banks will usually require you to take out property and liability insurance on your business and a personal life insurance policy on yourself naming the bank as beneficiary.

7. What if you can't get a bank loan?

A bank may come up with a variety of reasons for turning down your request for a loan. If you don't succeed at the first bank you try, go to others. There are plenty of banks around. It's a little easier in the U.S. than in Canada because the U.S. banking system is more competitive. In Canada, a handful of gigantic chartered banks have a virtual monopoly over banking, although you may have better luck at a credit union or trust company.

If you shop around and still can't get a bank loan, don't give up. There is a chance that government may lend you the money for your business.

b. GETTING A LOAN FROM GOVERNMENT

Preparing your case for a government loan or loan guarantee is not all that different from applying for a bank loan. You must provide the fullest possible documentation — cash flow statement, financial statements, personal resume — and be prepared to answer a lot of questions. You must also be prepared to provide collateral or security for your loan.

1. In the United States

Although some states have loan programs, the most promising government source of financial help for the small craft business is the United States Small Business Administration or SBA. The SBA has a loan guarantee program whereby a commercial bank loans you money and the SBA guarantees a substantial part of the loan. Direct SBA loans are available under a program for "economically and socially disadvantaged" businesses, primarily blacks, Native Americans and Spanish speaking people.

In order to qualify for an SBA loan or loan guarantee, a business must be unable to obtain financing from the private sector. In other words, you must be turned down by the banks before the SBA will lend you any money. The SBA makes or guarantees only about 30,000 loans a year, so they are relatively hard to get. There is a fairly long waiting period (usually four to six weeks) for the processing of an application. SBA loans also involve a lot of red tape, completing of forms and adherence to a set of operating guidelines which can limit your freedom and flexibility.

2. In Canada

Canada has a number of federal and provincial agencies that lend money to businesses, large and small.

At the federal level, the most promising source for a small craft business is the Federal Business Development Bank. The FBDB usually lends money to finance the purchase of new machinery and equipment. The officers of the FBDB can also give advice on a variety of other options for borrowing money from the government. In fact, you may not have to borrow all your financial requirements; there are a number of federal and provincial agencies that offer outright grants to businesses. (See section c. below.)

Many Canadian provinces have set up provincial Crown corporations that make loans to businesses. Contact your provincial department of development or commerce for details.

c. OTHER GOVERNMENT ASSISTANCE

In addition to loans and loan guarantees, other forms of aid may be available from governments. Government aid programs are complicated by the fact that some governments regard crafts as an educational or cultural field, while others see them primarily as an economic activity.

1. In the U.S.

The federal government provides financial assistance through the National Endowment for the Arts. These funds are not available directly to individuals but must be applied for through an arts or crafts organization. This type of assistance is more applicable to the artist-craftsperson or person producing one-of-a-kind pieces. For details, contact your state arts or crafts organization or the American Craft Council (see Appendix 1).

State assistance for small business varies from state to state; it is impossible to generalize for all 50 states. Some states, such as Connecticut, Massachusetts, and New Jersey have extensive programs for helping small business. Others, such as Delaware and Idaho, have few programs at all. Contact your state economic development agency for details on the programs available in your state. (See Appendix 2.)

2. In Canada

There is much more government assistance available to a crafts business in Canada than in the U.S. At the federal level, artists and craftspeople are eligible for direct grants from the Canada Council under a variety of different programs. Small craft businesses can receive financial assistance in the form of outright grants toward the cost of new buildings and equipment from the Department of Regional Industrial Expansion (DRIE).

There is a plethora of other federal assistance programs available. Many of them are applicable to a small craft business. The best way to find out about these programs is to ask your local office of the Federal Business Development Bank to send you their free booklet, *Assistance to Business in Canada (ABC)*. This booklet also has information to help you if you are a U.S. citizen who wishes to set up a business in Canada.

At the provincial level, a wide variety of aid programs are available to small businesses. These include loans, loan guarantees, outright grants for the purchase of new buildings and equipment, training programs for new employees, and marketing assistance programs. Some provinces, such as Nova Scotia, have financial assistance programs that will pay a portion of the costs of attending out-of-province trade shows and other marketing costs. To find out about these programs, write to your provincial department of industry or development. (See Appendix 2.)

d. CRAFTS ORGANIZATIONS

Crafts organizations can provide a number of useful services to the professional craftsperson. They are generally oriented toward the individual working alone rather than the small craft company with employees.

1. Marketing

Many crafts organizations run one or more retail fairs a year. Some provide wholesale opportunities for their members in the form of a register of producers that can be consulted by store owners. A few run craft fairs for wholesale buyers.

2. Other services

Some crafts organizations provide group insurance policies for their members. An organization may be able to offer assistance in the form of a loan or application for a grant for an individual craftsperson. National, state, and provincial crafts organizations can lobby governments on behalf of craftspeople.

There is a great need for this in the area of government procurement policies (such as the purchase of crafts for public buildings).

Crafts organizations can also help in the dissemination of information among craftspeople. Many organizations publish a newsletter or magazine and can provide lists of craft courses and suppliers of craft materials and craft books. They can also organize seminars on particular crafts (weaving, metalworking, pottery) or on aspects of craftwork in general (e.g., running a craft shop, marketing).

3. Some problems with crafts organizations

Most crafts organizations are composed of two distinct types of craftspeople. On the one side are the amateurs, part-time craft producers, and teachers. All these people earn their living in other ways than producing crafts for sale. On the other side are the professional craftspeople. Whether working singly or as owners of companies with employees, these people earn their living from crafts. The needs and interests of these two groups can be quite different.

Most professional craftspeople work long hours to make their businesses financially successful. They simply do not have the time to act as chairpersons on committees or to devote a lot of time to organizational work. As a result, a crafts organization may be run primarily by part-time craftspeople. Where this happens the interests of the full-time professional craftspeople may suffer. Examples of this are the use by a crafts organization of inappropriate standards for judging the quality of work or the scheduling of craft fairs without regard to the commercial buying season.

This situation is already changing as more and more craftspeople become professional. The effects of economic recession have also tended to make professional craftspeople more conscious of the advantages of belonging to an organization that can promote their group interests and lobby governments on their behalf. Professional craftspeople may become increasingly active in existing organizations or they may form their own separate organizations.

12

YOUR ACCOUNTING SYSTEM

a. WHAT KIND OF SYSTEM?

Bookkeeping. Ugh! That is the reaction of most craftspeople to the record-keeping side of their business. Keeping records is seen as an unpleasant distraction to the main business of making and selling their work. Most craftworkers would rather spend their time at the loom or the wheel than in the office.

While it may never become a joy to do, bookkeeping can be made more pleasant (or less unpleasant) by having a good system that you can readily understand. Moreover, a good bookkeeping system can be vital to the success of your business, letting you know at all times just how much money you are making.

There are two basic reasons for keeping accurate and up-to-date accounts.

Whether you like it or not, the tax department insists that you supply them with certain information at regular intervals — along with a slice of the business profits. Keeping adequate records is not only necessary to comply with the law but to ensure that you do not pay one single penny more in taxes than you have to.

A good bookkeeping system should tell you your exact financial position at all times. This will allow you to determine just how much money you are making and where your business is going. If you're heading for trouble, a good system will enable you to spot problems early and take corrective action before it is too late. Accurate records are also essential if your business needs to borrow money either for normal operating requirements or to finance expansion.

Do you need the services of a professional accountant? The answer to this should be no, at least in the beginning stages. Once your business is off and running, you will need an accountant about once a year, chiefly to advise you on your tax return, especially if your business is incorporated. But remember that first your business has to make money. If it doesn't, then you won't need books or an accountant at all. In the beginning, stay away from professional accountants who work out of large regional or national firms. Most of them know next to nothing about running a small business like yours, and they will charge you enormous fees for advice of little practical value.

What you need is a set of records that you can understand and maintain yourself. You may need help from a bookkeeper in setting it up and you would certainly be wise to have an accountant review your year-end tax return. But it will save you a lot of money if you can handle your own bookkeeping chores, at least in the beginning stages of your business. Later on, when your business is making lots of money, you can make your record-keeping system as sophisticated as you want.

56

The next chapter outlines a simple bookkeeping system for a small craft business. If you have a large number of customer accounts and this system becomes cumbersome, you can speed things up by using a "one write" accounting system. This essentially is a system that uses carbonized paper to post your sales automatically to a sales journal and ledger card. This can greatly save effort but most one write systems are fairly expensive, and you should not get involved with them until your business has reached the point where your accounting needs are clear.

Unless you choose to use a one write accounting system, the simple methods outlined in the following chapter should be perfectly adequate for a small craft business. They worked for our business from the beginning, when the annual sales were under $20,000 a year, right up to the point where sales were well over $200,000 at which point we put our entire record-keeping system on a microcomputer.

I would not advise using a one write system until I was very sure just how big my business was going to be. There is clearly a point in the development of your business where this simple manual system is too cumbersome and some kind of mechanization is called for, yet the situation does not really require a computer. If your business is operating with, say, one hundred or so active accounts and has perhaps two or three employees, you would probably benefit from a one write system. But if your business continues to grow (see chapter 15 on expanding your business) and you have substantially more than one hundred active accounts and more than five employees, you should explore the possibility of an accounting program that you can run on a microcomputer.

A few years ago, it would have been sheer folly for a small craft business to consider a computerized bookkeeping system. The available systems were terribly expensive and complex to understand and operate. The advent of inexpensive personal computers (microcomputers) and the recent explosion in the number of commercially available programs for microcomputers has changed all that. Small computerized accounting systems are now within the budget of the successful craft business.

It should be pointed out, however, that computerization is definitely not an area for the fainthearted and should certainly not be contemplated unless your business reaches a sufficient scale. There are no hard and fast rules of size to serve as guidelines here. Sometimes a craft business can generate $200,000 in sales with a few very large customer accounts; another business will have the same volume of sales with hundreds of small accounts. A very rough rule of thumb might be to consider computerization only when two or more of the following conditions hold for your business: sales exceed $200,000; you have more than five employees; you have more than 100 active customer accounts.

If you think your business could benefit from a computerized bookkeeping system, make sure that you investigate before you invest. Don't rush out and buy a machine (hardware) until you are absolutely sure that you have found the right accounting program (software). *Don't* be tempted to buy a "custom" program from someone who says he or she can write one just for you. Users of such programs always come to grief. There are a number of excellent commercially available accounting packages that can handle the accounting needs of the larger craft business.

b. SETTING UP A GOOD BOOKKEEPING SYSTEM

Setting up a good, inexpensive set of records for a craft business involves three things.

(a) Do as much of the basic bookkeeping work as possible yourself. It is a waste of money to ask your accountant to total invoices or to make journal entries for you. Do these things yourself. If your business grows to the point where you can't handle these chores, then consider handing them over to your spouse, a part-time bookkeeper or a microcomputer.

(b) Hand over the "higher-level" accounting functions and tax matters to your accountant. You should let your accountant show you how to set up and maintain your general ledger and either complete or review your year-end financial statements and income tax return.

(c) Always be up to date in your record-keeping. Never allow yourself to get so far behind that you are faced with a mountain of backlogged work and the task appears hopeless. Much of the onerous nature of bookkeeping work can be relieved if things are kept up to date. More importantly, not being up to date can mean that your records are not much use to you. During a critical phase of your business you will have to make decisions based on the latest information. Four or five month old data may not be of much use to you.

You should retain your bookkeeping records in your possession, except when your accountant is actually working on them. This applies especially to your general ledger. This is one of your most valuable business tools; it should be accessible to you at all times. You should not have to call up your accountant to get information that is in your general ledger.

One of the biggest problems our business encountered in expanding was in the control of labor costs. As our business grew, we incurred high costs training new employees. Our gross profit shrank to the point where we were actually losing money for a time; but it took several months before we were aware of the full extent of the problem.

We thought we had a good bookkeeping system and we did — up to a point. Our mistake was that we had engaged an outside bookkeeper to write up our general ledger and financial statements. The bookkeeper was first rate and did an excellent job, but because the general ledger was in her possession, we did not have the month-to-month figures to study during a critical phase in the growth of our business. Our financial statements were always two to three months behind. What we needed was immediate, up-to-date information on our gross profit from month to month.

Don't wait for formal financial statements at the end of the month, especially if your business is undergoing changes of any kind, e.g., expansion or development of new products. Get out your calculator and do a rough financial statement from the general ledger as soon as possible after the end of the month. Ask your accountant to show you how to do this.

The next chapter will show you a simple bookkeeping system for a small craft business.

13

KEEPING TRACK OF
YOUR INCOME AND EXPENSES

a. INCOME

You need to keep a record of all money received and, if you grant credit, a record of all money owing to you. When you sell your work at retail, either at craft markets or in your own store, make out a sales slip, and be sure to keep a carbon copy for yourself. Alternatively, you may enter the figures neatly in a ruled notebook. In either case, be sure to collect and record separately the state or provincial retail sales tax.

When you sell to shops, you should complete an invoice showing the customer's name and address, purchase order number, date of purchase, description and cost of goods, and any other charges, such as freight. Make sure that your terms of payment are stated clearly on the invoice form. Use standard blank invoice forms, which can be bought at most larger stationery stores, and rubber stamp them with your name, address, and terms of sale.

Buy blank invoice forms in triplicate. These can actually save you time. Send the original to the customer by mail under separate cover, send one copy as a packing slip with the goods, and keep one copy for your records. Invoices should be numbered consecutively, and your copies should be filed numerically so that they are easy to retrieve. (See Samples #5 and #6.)

In the beginning, when your needs are very limited, it is much better to buy all the forms you need ready made, but once you are using more than 100 or so a month it is cheaper to get them printed. Also it is much more convenient to have *invoices* and *order forms* custom printed with your items for sale preprinted. This saves an enormous amount of time in order taking and invoicing, but you can only use these types of forms when you have a reasonably stable product line.

It is always useful to leave a blank box somewhere on the order form and invoice form — sometimes a customer will have a special department number, or other special instructions and it is better to have a box to put it in rather than write it in the margin where it could be missed if you are thumbing through a batch of forms. (See the order form in Sample #7.)

If you sell all your work for cash on the barrelhead, you won't need to read the rest of this section at all. Chances are, however, that some of your sales to stores will be charge sales, so you will need some way of collecting from your customers.

At the end of the month, each customer should receive a statement of his or her account showing the outstanding balance. The easiest way to do this is to head up a ledger sheet for each customer, including the customer's address and credit limit. On this sheet record all invoices and payments together with their respective dates for that particular customer. These sheets have holes punched in them so that they can be bound together in alphabetical order — this is called your accounts receivable ledger. (See Sample #8.)

Your accounts receivable ledger is one of your most valuable business tools and should always be kept strictly up to date. It gives you a permanent listing of every one of your customer accounts and tells you the current status and amount of activity in each. At the end of the month, you simply copy the current balance onto one of the commercially available pre-printed statement forms. Choose a set of pre-printed statement forms that has at least two parts to it; send the original to the customer and keep a duplicate for your records. (See Samples #9 and #10.)

SAMPLE #5
PLAIN RUBBER STAMPED INVOICE

1034

ROCKINGHORSE CRAFTS LIMITED
Tantallon R.R. 2, Site 4, Box 7, N.S. B0J 3J0
Tel. (902) 835-5287 or 826-2272

SOLD TO

ABC Craft Shop
123 Main St.
Anytown, N.Y.

SHIP TO

DATE	SHIPPED VIA	FED. LICENCE NO.	PROV. LICENCE NO.	YOUR ORDER NO.	OUR ORDER NO.	TERMS	SALESMAN
May 25	UPS			1207	102	NET 30	

QUANTITY	DESCRIPTION	UNIT PRICE	AMOUNT
6	LG. BEAVER	9.50	57.00
12	SM. BEAVER	6.50	78.00
4	LG. SAINT BERNARD	47.50	190.00
12	BEAVER HAND PUPPET	8.00	96.00
	SUBTOTAL		421.00
	FREIGHT		21.50
	TOTAL		442.50
	6 PKG. Shipped May 25		

MOORE BUSINESS FORMS   3   7060E   MOORE BUSINESS FORMS 7S649E   E & OE

INVOICE

SAMPLE #6
CUSTOM PRINTED INVOICE

Rockinghorse Crafts Ltd.

INVOICE № 3653

Tantallon R.R. 2, Site 4, Box 7, N.S. B0J 3J0

Tel. (902) 835-5287 or 826-2272

SOLD TO

ABC Craft Shop
123 Main St.
Anytown, N.Y.

SHIP TO

Same

TERMS
NET 30 DAYS
2% per month interest on overdue accounts

Customer Order No.	Our Order No.	Shipped Via	Invoice Date	
1207	102	UPS	May 25	

Quantity	Description (size in inches)	Unit Price (Fed. Sales Tax incl.)	Amount	Quantity	Description (size in inches)	Unit Price (Fed. Sale Tax incl.)	Amount
	lg. Doctor Beaver 14 × 8				koala bear 5 × 9		
	lg. Eng. Beaver 14 × 8				rabbit 9 × 13		
6	lg. Beaver 14 × 8	9.50	57.00		raccoon (curled) 11 × 13		
	sm. Doctor Beaver 9 × 6				snuffi puppy 10 × 16		
	sm. Engineer Beaver 9 × 6			4	lg. Saint Bernard 19 × 36	47.50	190.00
	sm. Billy Beaver 9 × 6				sm. Saint Bernard 14 × 24		
12	sm. Beaver 9 × 6	6.50	78.00		lg. teddy bear 21		
	baby seal 5 × 10				sm. teddy bear 18		
	sm. brown bear 10 × 14				cat pillow pal 12 × 15		
	med. brown bear 20 × 15				elephant pillow pal 12 × 15		
	lg. brown bear 36 × 30				lamb pillow pal 12 × 15		
	elephant 11 × 13				lion pillow pal 13 × 13		
	fox (curled) 9 × 12			12	beaver puppet	8.00	96.00
	lg. hedgehog (lying) 5 × 7				red fox puppet		
	sm. hedgehog (lying) 4 × 5				rabbit puppet		
	hedgehog (sitting) 5 × 9				raccoon puppet		
	lamb 14 × 14				lamb puppet		
	polar bear 12 × 20						

Total (less shipping) 421.00

Doctor Beaver books ....

Prepaid Transportation Charges 21.50

TOTAL 442.50

Tax No.	No. of Packages	Weight	Date Shipped	Order Complete	Balance Cancelled	Balance to Follow
	6	100	May 25	✓		

No claims can be considered subsequent to 7 days after delivery.

ROCKINGHORSE CRAFTS

Mailing address: Tantallon R.R. 2, Site 4, Box 7, Halifax County, Nova Scotia, Canada, B0J 3J0
Telephone 1-902-835-5287 or 826-2272
DOCTOR BEAVER'S FRIENDS   FURRY TOY ANIMALS

WHOLESALE PRICE LIST - ORDER FORM
(effective Oct. 15, 1983)

Date required	Cust. PO #	SOLD TO
SAP	**18623**	**Bestmade Crafts**
Ship via		**180 The Mall**
POST		**Supercity, N.J.**

Shipping address (if different):
Same

QTY	#	DESCRIPTION	UNIT COST	TOTAL	QTY	#	DESCRIPTION	UNIT COST	TOTAL
		BEAVERS					**HEDGEHOGS**		
	101	lg. Dr. beaver	12.75		1	501	sm. lying	3.60	
2	102	lg. eng. beaver	11.75		1	502	lg. lying	4.25	
2	103	lg. beaver	9.75						
2	104	sm. Dr. Beaver	8.50			503	chicken	2.50	
4	105	sm. eng. beaver	8.25			505	fox (curled)	9.00	
	106	sm. Billy Beaver	8.25		4	506	lamb (lying)	8.50	
4	108	sm. beaver	6.75			507	raccoon	10.75	
					2	508	rabbit	9.00	
		BEARS				509	leopard	47.50	
	203	sitting panda	12.75						
	204	lying panda	12.75				**PILLOW PALS**		
						601	cat	6.25	
		TEDDY BEARS			4	602	lamb	6.25	
4	301	sm. white teddy	6.50		4	603	lion	6.25	
2	302	med. white teddy	9.75			604	duck (small)	2.80	
1	303	lg. white teddy	12.75						
							HAND PUPPETS		
	304	sm. brown teddy	6.50		4	701	beaver	8.25	
	305	med. brown teddy	9.75		6	702	lamb	8.25	
	306	lg. brown teddy	12.75		6	703	rabbit	8.25	
					2	704	raccoon	9.75	
		DOGS			2	705	terrier	7.25	
2	401	sm. terrier	8.25			706	duck	7.25	
2	402	med.terrier	10.75			707	teddy bear	7.25	
1	403	lg. terrier	19.75						
4	404	"Snuffy" puppy	10.75			801	BILLY BEAVER BOOKS		
2	405	sm. St. Bernard	25.75				cost $1.75		
1	406	lg. St. Bernard	48.00				retail $2.95		

PRICES and SPECIFICATIONS are subject to change without notice
TERMS: NET 30 days with approved credit or prepaid
MINIMUM ORDER: $100.
DELIVERY: 2 - 3 wks.

_____
Buyer's Signature

SAMPLE #8
ACCOUNTS RECEIVABLE LEDGER

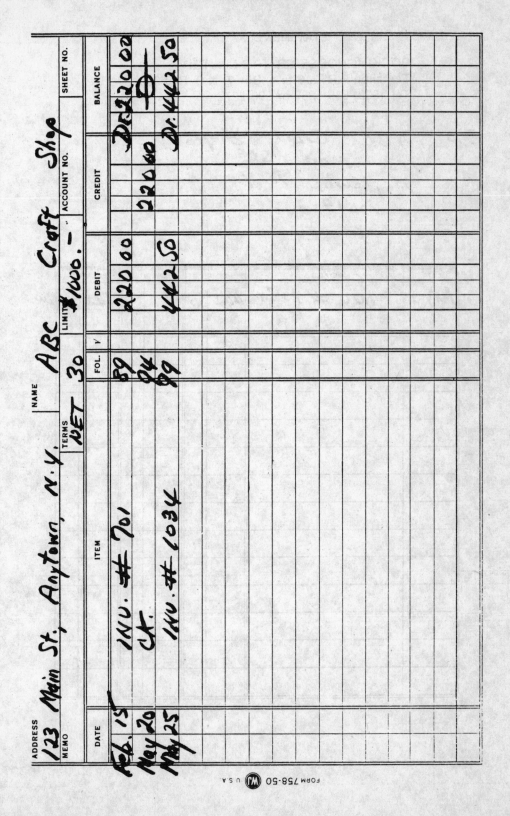

ADDRESS 123 Main St., Anytown, N.Y.

NAME ABC Craft Shop

TERMS NET 30

LIMIT $1000.-

ACCOUNT NO.

SHEET NO.

DATE	ITEM	MEMO	FOL.	√	DEBIT	CREDIT	BALANCE
Feb. 1st	Inv. # 701		82		220 00		Dr 220 00
May 20	Ct.		84			220 00	-0-
May 25	Inv. # 1034		99		442 50		Dr. 442 50

FORM 758-50 Ⓦ U.S.A.

63

SAMPLE #9
PLAIN RUBBER STAMPED STATEMENT

STATEMENT

ROCKINGHORSE CRAFTS LIMITED
Tantallon R.R. 2, Site 4, Box 7, N.S. B0J 3J0
Tel. (902) 835-5287 or 826-2272

To: ABC Craft Shop.
123 Main St.
Anytown, N.Y.
10019

DATE	DETAILS	DEBIT		CREDIT		BALANCE		
May 15	INV. #1034	442	50			442	50	DR

SAMPLE #10
CUSTOM PRINTED STATEMENT

STATEMENT

Rockinghorse Crafts Ltd.

Tantallon R.R. 2, Site 4, Box 7, N.S. B0J 3J0

Tel. (902) 835-5287

TERMS
NET 30 DAYS
2% per month
interest on
overdue accounts

DATE _____

ABC Craft Shop
123 Main St.
Anytown N.Y.
10019

DATE	DETAILS	DEBIT		CREDIT		BALANCE		
May 25	INV.# 1034	442	50			442	50	Dr.

As your business grows, it is possible to modify this system. If you have a large number of accounts and the system becomes cumbersome, you can speed things up by using the one write accounting system mentioned in the previous chapter.

You should deposit all cash and checks as soon as possible after they are received. When a customer sends payment for goods shipped on account, be sure to record his or her name in your deposit book alongside the amount so that the account can be correctly credited. Mistakes here can be costly in terms of lost customer goodwill.

b. EXPENSES

Keep a detailed record of all your expenses as they occur. Don't rely on your memory to recall amounts that you have paid out. Always ask for receipts. At times this is a nuisance, but you *must* do it if you want the expenditure to count as a business expense. In those few cases where it is not possible to get a receipt, e.g., parking, jot down the expense in your notebook.

If you attend an out of town craft show, bring an envelope with you and stuff into it your receipts for meals, hotel bills, gas, etc. When you get back home, you can sort out the different kinds of expenses and write yourself a business check for those items that you have paid for out of cash from your own pocket.

Whenever possible, pay your bills by check so that your canceled checks can serve as receipts. Retain all your suppliers' invoices. File these away alphabetically in an accordion file or in file folders so that you can retrieve them easily if you want to verify expenses, check supplier prices, terms, etc.

c. MAKING JOURNAL ENTRIES

Your system will be simpler if you keep all your figures in one big journal. I know many books on accounting refer to sales journals, cash disbursement journals, and others, but it is simpler and easier for a small craft business to keep everything in one big journal. (Accountants call this the synoptic journal, but the name doesn't really matter.) Be sure to buy a big one with at least 24 columns across; 30 columns is even better if you can get it.

Sample #11 shows how to head the columns and how to enter information in such a journal. As you can see, each amount is entered twice, once as a credit and once as a debit. No matter how many entries you make, the sum of the debit and credit entries should always be equal, providing you with an automatic check on the accuracy of your figures.

In our illustration we do not enter cash (i.e., recognize it in our system) until it is deposited in the bank. Each of the major income and expense items has a column of its own. We have entered only a few; you can have as many as you like, e.g., truck, operating supplies.

To understand the meaning of debits and credits, think of each transaction as involving a side that "gives" and a side that "receives" something. A debit entry is made in the account that receives and a credit entry is made in the account that gives. The first transaction in Sample #11 is a cash sale, the results of a craft market. In it the bank receives — is debited with — $550 which is given by — is credited to — sales ($500) and sales tax ($50).

The other transactions are described underneath the sample.

Don't despair if you don't grasp the nature of debits and credits the first time around. Before entering into business, I had steeped myself thoroughly in the liberal arts (philosophy and history) and totally ignored the crass world of commerce. I thought debits and credits were some kind of breakfast cereal. But it didn't take me long to find out otherwise.

Once you've made a few entries (especially when using real money for practice) you'll quickly get the hang of it, and soon you'll begin to wonder why they never taught it to you at school.

d. DEPRECIATION

If you buy an important piece of equipment or make an addition to your workshop, you make a special kind of entry in your records. Real property and equipment constitute fixed assets. These are not used or consumed in the same way as your materials, but a part of their useful life goes into the production of each one of your products. It would not be realistic to consider the whole cost of a fixed asset as an expense in any one year. Instead, the cost of the asset is distributed over the period of its useful life. This is known as depreciation of the asset. Your electric kiln, wood lathe or loom as well as your workshop, vehicle, and other fixed assets will last only a certain number of years. At the end of that time, you will have to replace them.

Depreciation is an important factor in calculating your year-end profit and income tax. For income tax purposes various kinds of fixed assets are grouped together in classes and yearly depreciation is allowed at a certain prescribed rate by the tax department. Certain types of production equipment can, for example, be written off in a year or two.

Yearly depreciation rates for the most common types of fixed assets are available from the tax department (the IRS or Revenue Canada) or you can get them from your accountant. The amount that you choose to write off in your yearly financial statement may be different from the amount used for income tax purposes. This is a highly complex subject beyond the scope of this book; seek the advice of your accountant.

e. PAYROLL

If you are employing others or if your business is incorporated, you are responsible for deductions at source from your employees' wages or salaries. You must open an account with the tax department and they will send you a book of tables of the amounts that you must deduct for each pay period. To keep track of this you should use a separate payroll book with columns for the various types of deductions. These are available in different sizes in most good stationery stores. For the regulations pertaining to payroll taxes in the U.S. and Canada, see chapter 10.

SAMPLE #11
JOURNAL

MAY 198-

DATE	DESCRIPTION	CK. #S	BANK DR.	BANK CR.	A/C RECEIVABLE DR.	A/C RECEIVABLE CR.	SALES CR.	SALES TAX CR.	FREIGHT DR.	FREIGHT CR.	PURCHASES DR.	OFFICE SUPPLIES DR.	A/C PAYABLE DR.	A/C PAYABLE CR.
MAY 2	1. Riverside Craft Market		550.00				500.00	50.00						
MAY 2	2. ABC Shop				250.00		240.00			10.00				
MAY 5	3. Zy Shop		175.00			175.00								
MAY 7	4. Fleecy Wool Co.										120.00			120.00
MAY 8	5. Jill's Stationery	89		45.00								45.00		

1. You make a cash sale. The bank is debited with $550; $500 is credited to sales and $50 is credited to sales tax.

2. You sell a customer goods on credit. Accounts receivable is debited with $250; sales is credited with $240 and freight (which you paid for but intend to charge to the customer) is credited with $10.

3. A customer pays you $175 for goods you shipped last month. You debit the bank with $175 and credit accounts receivable with $175.

4. You buy $120 worth of raw materials on credit. You debit purchases with $120 and credit accounts payable with $120.

5. You pay (by check) a $45 bill for stationery supplies you received on credit last month. You debit accounts payable with $45 and credit bank with $45.

f. THE GENERAL LEDGER

Each of the columns in your journal will have a separate account or page in your general ledger. Entries in the general ledger are usually made at the end of each month, and it is a good idea for you to learn to do this yourself. It is advisable, however, for you to get your accountant to set up the general ledger for you in the beginning and to explain to you how financial statements are taken off. This may involve several fairly lengthy sessions with your accountant, but it is worthwhile. In the long run you will save money. By having a complete understanding of your financial records, you will be able to make your business run more efficiently and make bigger profits.

For more details about how to set up your own books, see *Basic Accounting for the Small Business,* another title in the Self-Counsel Series.

g. TAXES

We have already looked at the reasons for keeping accurate and up to date records and some of the mechanics of record-keeping. As mentioned earlier, one of the main reasons for having a good bookkeeping system is to avoid paying any more taxes than you absolutely have to.

Since the tax laws are not only extremely complex but are constantly being changed, it is absolutely necessary for the small businessperson to seek tax advice from a competent public accountant. However, just as in the area of record-keeping, there are quite a number of things that you can do yourself to reduce the tax bite.

1. Income

In the area of what to include as income there is not much scope for tax saving. Not declaring income earned from your business is tax fraud pure and simple. Apart from being illegal, not declaring income can be highly disadvantageous if you are applying for a loan. There may come a time when the continued success or even survival of your business will depend on getting a loan. No respectable lender will give you money on the basis of your word that your financial records have to be seen in the light of the extra income you do not declare on your tax return!

A similar situation would arise if you wanted to sell your business; you can't seriously expect a potential buyer to offer a big price for your business on the basis that you cheat on your income tax.

2. Expenses

In the area of expenses, there is more scope for tax saving. Keep receipts for *all* business expenses *and* personal expenses where any portion of the expense can be charged off to your business. Though simple and obvious, this rule is often ignored either because people find it too much trouble to ask for receipts or because they believe that certain expenses will be allowed without them.

If it is not too much trouble earning your income in the first place, it certainly isn't too much trouble to ask for a receipt. It's this simple: every time you keep the receipt for $2 spent on postage or parking or whatever, you put another tax-free dollar into your pocket.

There are very few places where you simply cannot get a receipt for expenditures. Where this does happen, as in the case of pay telephones or parking meters, you should keep a diary of these expenses. I said this earlier, but it bears repeating. You would be surprised how some of these minor expenses can add up to quite significant amounts in a year's time.

If you believe that you are entitled to claim certain expenses without substantiating receipts, you are completely wrong. Your mistake could turn out to be a costly one. *Without receipts a tax assessor does not have to allow a single red cent for your expenses, no matter what they are.* In the case of relatively small amounts paid for by cash, you must be particularly careful. While on a sales trip or attending an out of town craft market, always ask for and keep all your receipts for meals and lodging. Keep a detailed diary of expenses for parking, postage, pay telephone, and similar small amounts.

(a) Automobile expenses

Both the IRS and Revenue Canada require that all vehicle expenses be recorded and kept. It is not sufficient just to write down expenses incurred when you were actually using the vehicle for business. You must keep the entire year's expenses, including fuel, repairs, insurance, parking, depreciation, interest on the vehicle loan, license, and registration fees. If you use your vehicle for both business and pleasure, you then allocate the total vehicle expenses to your business on the basis of business miles travelled to total miles travelled.

(b) Business expenses in the home

One of the many advantages of operating your craft business from your home is the ability to deduct a certain portion of your home expenses, such as heat, rent, taxes, utilities, and mortgage. In Canada, mortgage interest payments are not normally deductible for private residences, so anything you can do to make a portion deductible will result in significant tax benefits.

In order to deduct a portion of your home expenses, you are required to establish that you regularly use a specific part of the home for your craft business. Once this is established, you can deduct the portion of items, such as rent, heat, etc., assignable to that portion of the home. But be careful here. In order to qualify for a tax deduction, a room must be used solely for business purposes. You cannot, for example, claim office expenses for an "office" that occupies a part of your bedroom.

(c) Maintenance and repairs

Maintenance refers to the routine painting of a building or replacement of parts on machinery and equipment. Repairs means fixing a breakdown or restoring something to normal mechanical condition. The value of a repair can be claimed as a business expense in the year it was incurred.

But what happens in the case of very extensive repairs? If you have a flat roof that leaks, you may decide that rather than have it patched up, you will have a pitched roof built over the building. In this case, there will be an addition to the building, even though it was prompted by the need for a repair.

The difference from the tax point of view is that a repair can be claimed as an expense in the current year, while an addition has to be added to the capital cost of the asset and depreciated over a number of years. Also, if the addition is depreciated and the asset is subsequently sold for more than the depreciated value, there is a "recapture" of depreciation and tax has to be paid on the recapture. (See page 67 on depreciation.)

Naturally it is to your advantage as a taxpayer to "expense" an item whenever possible. If in doubt about whether an item can be treated this way, check with your accountant.

3. Profits

There are numerous possibilities for tax savings in the way you handle the profits from your craft business. If you are operating your business under your own name, all the profits of the business are considered to be your income and they are taxed in your name. It is possible, as mentioned elsewhere, to split the income from your business among family members by putting your spouse and children on the payroll. Chapter 14 discusses the various forms of business organization and suggests ways of saving taxes by splitting income among family members.

Say you want to take out $28,000 in salary from your business in a given year. The tax bite is obviously much less if you and your spouse each take $14,000. But in order to take full advantage of these tax saving possibilities, certain conditions must be met. (See chapter 14.)

If your business is incorporated, there are further possibilities of tax saving. Because you and your company are separate and distinct legal entities, it is possible to leave a portion of your profits in the company to use for whatever company purpose you choose. However, this only saves taxes when the corporate rate of taxation is less than your personal rate. This is frequently the case in Canada where small, Canadian-owned private corporations that meet certain conditions are entitled to special tax rates of 15% to 27%. (Also in Canada there is a further 5% reduction in the corporate tax rate for manufacturers, which includes almost all craft businesses.)

Instead of withdrawing money from your company in the form of salaries for yourself or other members of your family, it is possible to take money out of the company in the form of dividends. But there is also a disadvantage to this. Since dividends are now subject to taxes in both the U.S. and Canada, the net effect is that these withdrawals are subject to double taxation — once when the company earns the money and once again when the money is paid out. However, in certain circumstances, it is still advantageous from a tax point of view to withdraw money from your company in the form of dividends. But check first with your accountant.

When it comes to income tax advice, don't rely on bookkeepers. Their expertise is limited to the organization of information into the standard accounting forms. For tax matters you should seek the services of a qualified professional accountant who can advise you how to minimize tax payable and maximize profit in light of the most recent rules and regulations. These rules and regulations are not only highly complex, they are constantly changing.

What you can do, however, to minimize the accounting fee is to have all your bookkeeping done so that you pay for high-priced accounting and tax advice only where it is needed. You can also be aware of the various possibilities for tax saving as outlined above so that you can ask specific questions of your accountant about what is best in your particular circumstances.

Choosing an accountant is as important as choosing your doctor or lawyer. You want someone with a good professional reputation who also makes you feel comfortable. Avoid anyone who can converse only in unintelligible accountant's jargon or who bills you for a telephone conference if you call to clarify a minor point on the telephone. Look for a professional who regularly deals with and understands the needs of small businesses and is prepared to help you set up a simple system along the lines recommended in this chapter.

If you don't know where to start looking, ask your bank manager or a business acquaintance if they can recommend someone. Don't be afraid to talk to several accountants before making a choice and don't hesitate to ask about their fees. A good accountant can actually save you far more than his or her fee but that doesn't mean you don't need to know the size of the fee in advance.

14

MANAGING YOUR CRAFT BUSINESS

a. BUSINESS ORGANIZATION

The form of organization of your craft business is not likely to occupy a lot of your time in the beginning. Nor should it. There are more important things to do like getting your business off and running. Before too long, however, you should give some thought to the structure of your business.

The main reason for this is that it allows you to plan for the future. This planning will provide for the easy development of your business. As your income rises, you may want to expand your business, perhaps employing assistants or enlarging your workshop. These moves can lead to increased capital or production costs, which can be very hard to handle for a business that is not organized.

There are three possible forms of organization for a small craft business. Your business may be run as a sole proprietorship, a partnership or an incorporated company.

1. The sole proprietorship

Most small craft businesses operate as sole proprietorships. This is the simplest form of business organization. No legal papers are required, there are no extra expenses, you have only yourself to blame if things go wrong, and you take all the profits if you succeed. The tax consequences are also the simplest. Whatever the business makes is counted as your personal income, and you pay taxes on it accordingly.

A sole proprietorship can be operated legally under your own name without registration. But if you want to adopt a distinctive name for your business, as many craftspeople do, it is advisable to register it. This is a very simple procedure. For the specific requirements in your locality, contact the county clerk's office or provincial companies office.

2. The partnership

A partnership is a slightly more complex form of business organization than the sole proprietorship. Legal expenses are minimal, but a partnership should include a written agreement with your partner, which should then be registered as a proper legal document.

Sometimes partnerships work out extremely well, especially when each partner brings specific expertise or skills to the business that the other partner lacks. A good combination could be that of a skilled designer/craftsperson together with someone who has a flair for marketing. On the other hand, many partnerships fail because of personality conflicts, differing goals and ambitions, and inadequate written agreements.

A fertile area for disagreements between craft business partners is the size of the business. As a craft business grows, one of the partners may feel that the commercial side of the operation tends to overshadow the creative, artistic side. This is a frequent conflict when partners have different goals for the business.

A major drawback to the partnership form of organization is that each partner assumes unlimited liability for all debts incurred in the business. This means unlimited personal liability. In other words, should the business fail, creditors can claim against the personal assets of one or all of the partners.

3. The corporation

A corporation is a separate, legal entity. Setting it up involves some paperwork and incorporation fees and may require legal help. The rules of incorporation vary in different states and provinces in the degree of complexity, the number of persons required to form a corporation, and the costs. Some states and provinces permit an individual to incorporate. "Incorporation kits" are available which permit you to do much of the legal work yourself and greatly reduce the cost of incorporating.

One of the biggest advantages of the corporate form is the limited liability of the shareholder for debts of the company. Each shareholder's liability is limited to the amount of money individually invested. Creditors of the company have no claims against the personal assets of shareholders.

In actual practice, however, not all of the advantages of limited liability are available to the small corporation. Where loans to the company are involved, banks and other financial institutions may require that owners or shareholders provide personal guarantees. This in effect nullifies the advantages of limited liability as far as your obligations to the bank are concerned.

There are some tax advantages to the corporate form of business organization. You do not need to incorporate to be able to deduct a salary paid to your spouse, but by incorporating it is possible to pay wages or salaries to other members of your family as well. However, you must be able to show that they performed specific duties and that the remuneration paid was reasonable. We shall deal with this in a later section.

A craftsperson can withdraw money either as salary/wages or in the form of dividends. As income rises and the person's marginal rate of taxation increases, it is sometimes advantageous to withdraw money from the company in the form of dividends where the effective rate of taxation is less than it would be if the money were taxed as salary. This is a highly complex area and before making a decision about incorporating, it is best to seek the advice of a tax accountant.

b. FINANCIAL PLANNING

To manage your craft business efficiently you must be certain that you have enough cash on hand for your day-to-day operations. You may have a good product and sales that have grown to the point where you hired an assistant, but still find yourself chronically short of ready cash to pay your bills or to withdraw sufficient money for your personal needs.

Cash management is relatively simple if all your sales are on a cash basis. If you sell $5,000 worth of products in May, you know you will receive $5,000 the same month. If, however, a large part of your business is done on credit, you would not receive the $5,000 until some later time. How much later would depend on your credit terms and the extent to which your customers adhere to them. If you have a large financial commitment to meet in May, say a down payment on a new piece of equipment, you will need to know just how much cash you can expect to come in during May. You need to prepare a cash flow statement.

A cash flow statement is simply a way of setting out clearly the timing and amounts of cash income and cash payments. A typical cash flow statement for a craft business might look like the one in Sample #12. This is for the period from May to the end of the year. (Any time period can be chosen.) We have also shown projected financial transactions, i.e., how much the business will have to borrow and when it will be able to repay its operating loans. This is the kind of information you would need to provide to a banker when applying for a loan. (See chapter 11 on how to apply for a bank loan.)

c. GIVING CREDIT TO YOUR CUSTOMERS

At some point, you will have to face the question of whether to grant credit to your customers. Most production craft businesses do grant credit, and you may have to follow suit if you want to remain competitive. The main advantage of granting credit is that it increases sales by allowing goods to be purchased by retailers who would otherwise be unable to do so. This in turn helps the retailers to buy a little extra and thereby increase their own sales.

The disadvantage of credit granting is that you are in effect giving a loan to the customer. You incur all the costs of production but you do not receive payment until some time later. This means you must have more capital available than if you did business strictly on a cash basis. In addition, there are the costs of keeping records, billing, and collecting your money. There is also the possibility that some customers won't pay and you will end up with a bad debt expense.

If you decide to grant credit to your customers, you should try to minimize the disadvantages by doing the following:

(a) Make sure that the costs of granting credit are built into your prices. This will be difficult to do exactly, but you should estimate the various

SAMPLE #12
CASH FLOW STATEMENT

BEST MADE WOOD CRAFT CO. INC.

CASH FLOW PROJECTIONS AND PROJECTED FINANCIAL TRANSACTIONS

	1	2	3	4	5	6	7	8
	MAY	JUNE	JULY	AUGUST	SEPT.	OCT.	NOV.	DEC.
1 Sales	18,000	20,000	22,000	18,000	18,000	29,000	29,000	20,000
2 Collections on account	14,500	16,000	19,000	21,000	20,000	27,000	28,000	20,000
3 Other cash receipts	3,400	1,400	1,400	1,400	440	440	440	440
4 Total cash receipts	17,900	17,400	20,400	22,400	20,440	27,440	28,440	20,440
5 Purchases	10,000	4,000	4,000	4,000	4,000	4,000	4,000	4,000
6 Wages & Salaries	6,000	6,800	6,800	6,800	6,800	6,800	6,800	6,800
7 Accounting	100	100	100	100	100	100	100	100
8 Advertising & Shows	1,500	1,100						
9 Electricity	125	140	140	140	140	140	140	140
10 Fuel	100	75	50	50	50	75	100	100
11 Insurance (paid in 2 installments)	1,250	1,250						
12 Interest (long term)	708	708	708	708	708	708	708	708
13 Operating supplies	300	300	300	300	300	400	400	300
14 Repairs & maintenance	200	200	200	200	200	200	200	200
15 Taxes	200	200	200	200	200	200	200	200
16 Telephone	90	90	90	90	90	90	90	90
17 Truck	200	200	200	200	200	200	200	200
18 Sales taxes	1,260	1,620	1,800	1,980	1,620	1,620	2,610	2,610
19 Pre-paid freight	720	800	880	720	720	1,160	1,160	800
20 Sales staff commissions	450	2,100	2,490	2,460	2,160	2,250	2,400	2,400
21 Bank loan interest	140	210	247	227	178	136	25	—
22 Total monthly expenses	23,343	19,893	18,205	18,175	17,466	18,079	19,133	18,648
23 Net monthly cash surplus [deficit]	[5443]	[2,493]	2,195	4,225	2,974	9,361	9,307	1,792
24 Borrowing to maintain $1,000 min. bal.	6,000	3,000	—	0	—	—	—	—
25 Cumulative borrowing ($11,000 at end of April)	17,000	20,000	18,000	14,000	11,000	2,000	—	—

extra costs, particularly paperwork, involved in credit sales and factor these into your prices.

(b) The risks of granting credit can be greatly reduced by establishing a set of rules and sticking strictly to them. Decide what terms you will offer and who will qualify for credit.

Net 30 days is the most common payment period in the craft/giftware business. You may want to offer a discount for cash payment or for payment within 10 days. You must also decide what action you will take if accounts become overdue and what interest rate you will charge. Both rates for discounts and interest charge penalties should be slightly higher than the current rate you are paying to your bank for commercial loans.

The best way to establish the creditworthiness of new customers is to ask them to fill out a credit questionnaire. This need be no more than a typewritten sheet, which you can have photocopied. It should include space for their name, address and telephone number, length of time at that address, bank name and address, and credit references You should ask for the names of at least three suppliers with whom the customer is currently doing business.

Make sure you take the time to check out a customer's supplier references. You must find out the length of time the supplier has been doing business with the customer, the size of the customer's credit limit, the supplier's credit terms, and the past pattern of payments by the customer. This can be done by mail or over the telephone. If your customer is in a big hurry, then you should request payment in advance for the first order or permission to ship the order C.O.D.

To make your credit system work properly, you must have an efficient invoicing and billing system (see chapter 13). If you neglect to send out bills, some of your customers are almost certain to neglect to send in their payments. Your accounts receivable should be monitored regularly to detect those that have become overdue. A prompt reminder to a delinquent account will usually get you a payment. Where this does not happen, you should get on the telephone and find out why.

Be tactful and polite but at the same time firm in your collection call. Perhaps your customer has simply forgotten to pay. In most instances your call will prompt the customer to pay. Where this does not bring the desired result, you ought to consider handing the account over to a collection agency. But do this only as a last resort if all other efforts to collect the account fail. The best way to protect yourself against the risk of non-payment is to have a sound credit policy to begin with and to carry out detailed credit checks on your customers.

For more information on this topic, see *Collection Techniques for the Small Business*, another title in the Self-Counsel Series.

d. INSURANCE

Insurance is one of the things that you cannot afford to be without. If you and your family are dependent upon the earnings from your craft business, you should provide yourself with as much protection as possible.

You are certainly going to need fire and theft coverage on your building, tools, and inventory. As your inventory is likely to fluctuate from month to month, it is a good idea to investigate a stock coverage policy that allows for these fluctuations. With this kind of coverage your premiums for insurance on your stock reflect the amount of inventory actually on hand at the end of each month.

Third party insurance is also necessary, particularly if you have a retail operation. This will protect you if a lawsuit arises out of an injury that someone sustains on your premises and for which you might be held responsible. You ought also to consider insurance to protect you against suits that could arise from product defects.

You should also have insurance against loss of income that may result from an interruption in your business due to some unforeseen disaster. Disability insurance will cover you for any permanent injury.

Life insurance has been described as a way of keeping you poor all your life so that you can die rich. Nonetheless, you should seriously consider at least some life insurance if you have a family; more can be added as your income grows. Endowment insurance will pay the whole amount of the policy directly to you if you survive beyond a specified date or to your beneficiary if you die before that time. This kind of insurance can also serve as collateral for a loan.

Insurance is expensive. You should shop around for it like you would for anything else. Use an insurance agent who deals with many different insurance companies and who will spend some time with you going over your needs and checking with the various companies on prices.

If you are operating a craft business at home, tell your insurance agent. Don't assume that your home or tenant policy will cover your business assets for loss by fire or theft. Not informing your insurance company that you are carrying on a business in your house could also invalidate your home policy.

e. YOUR CRAFT BUSINESS AND YOUR FAMILY

Going into business for yourself involves not just a job but a particular lifestyle. You have much greater freedom of choice than the person who is employed by someone else. You control your hours of work and working conditions, and you must regularly make decisions about matters most people take for granted. You are more likely to succeed in your own business if you are the type of person who enjoys decision-making. You also need to be able to live sensibly with your greater freedom, neither wasting your time nor wearing yourself out with too much work.

We have already mentioned the many advantages of working at home; however, working at home calls for more self-discipline than if you went out to work. You are responsible to yourself. You can work at any time of the day or night. *But* your craft business must coexist with the other members of your family.

If your family is not directly involved in your business and your work at home, you will have to make it clear that when you are at work you are not available for family chores. You should set aside certain hours of the day when you are at work in your studio or workshop; during that time it should be understood that you are not to be disturbed.

It may be possible to involve your family in your business. One of the unique features of a craft business is the way in which it can lend itself to family participation. Sometimes both partners are involved directly in craft design and production. Or, if only one partner is actually producing, the spouse can be of assistance selling at craft markets, running your own retail outlet or doing the books.

Your children can help out at craft markets and at a variety of jobs around the workshop. Even quite young children can be of assistance in the workshop — if your family gets along well together. Two of our children regularly perform a variety of jobs in our business: selling at markets, cleaning the workshop, stuffing envelopes, filling boxes. They also make their own hooked rugs, which we sell as a sideline at craft markets.

If you are employing your spouse and/or children regularly, part of the income from your craft business can be split among family members, thereby lessening your tax burden. Be careful, however, to pay family members in proportion to what they actually do. Amounts paid to your spouse and children must be reasonable or they will not be allowed by the tax department. As a general rule, you should pay members of your family the same amounts you would have to pay hired help to do the same jobs. Also make certain that you pay them at regular intervals and that they have their own bank accounts.

In some cases, it may be necessary to give members of your family specific training so that you can take advantage of the opportunity of employing them in your business. We taught two of our children rug hooking so that at a relatively early age they were capable of earning substantial sums of money from our business. Depending on where you live, children can receive up to several thousand dollars of income annually tax free and you can still claim an exemption for them on your income tax return.

All this is only worthwhile, however, if your family enjoys it. Some craftspeople can't bear to have their children around them while they work. The concept of the family as an economic unit working together is not particularly well entrenched in most segments of contemporary North American society. The extent to which your spouse and/or children should get involved in your craft business will depend very much on how closely knit your family is.

15

EXPANDING YOUR CRAFT BUSINESS

a. HOW BIG DO YOU WANT TO BE?

We have already mentioned the tremendous variety possible in the craft world. In effect you can be as small or as big as you wish. Just how big can you be? Well, if the conditions are right, i.e., you have a really good product and the entrepreneurial ability to develop and market it, you can build your craft business into a substantial company with hundreds of employees and sales in the millions.

There are literally thousands of firms today that are essentially craft businesses, though we tend generally not to think of them as such. Most of the famous British and European potteries, for example, are large-scale craft industries. In North America, there are thousands of handcraft companies making everything from alligator purses to ornamental zarfs. (Incidentally, a zarf is a metal cup-shaped holder used to hold a hot coffee cup.) Some of these are well known, others less so. Many of them would rank as substantial enterprises anywhere in terms of sales and employment figures.

However, the vast majority of craft businesses are small, consisting of just the owner and sometimes one or two employees. The owners of most small craft businesses prefer to keep them that way. Building a large enterprise means taking a lot of risks. It also involves a completely different lifestyle. In the small craft enterprise, even where there are employees, the owner/manager generally works right in the studio along with everyone else. In a larger operation, the owner/manager would most probably not be involved directly in the production side of the operation.

Whether a particular craft business can operate on a greatly increased scale depends on a variety of factors. One of the most important is the product itself. Unless the product has some inherent features that distinguish it as a handmade piece, it will not be able to compete in the marketplace either with domestic factory-made goods or cheap (largely handmade) imported goods. There is no one single identifying feature that gives a product this characteristic, handcrafted appeal. It may lie in the exceptionally high quality of the work, the obvious attention to detail, the intricacy or beauty of the design or even the buyer's knowledge that the piece was made by hand rather than turned out by a machine.

If you think it is possible for you to sell vastly greater quantities of your product and you personally are prepared to go into large scale production, there are some things you should investigate first. We shall look at each of these below.

1. Rate of growth

Look at the rate of growth of your business to date. In a small craft business, it is not uncommon to have growth rates of 200 or 300% or even higher in the first few years. But be careful to view this in the proper perspective. You started out very small, perhaps part-time. It is much easier to achieve a given percentage increase on a smaller base. If first year sales from your part-time business were $10,000, you would only need to sell another $10,000 worth of products to double your sales. If you are selling $50,000 worth, you obviously need a much larger absolute increase in business in order to double your sales. A fairly obvious point, but you'd be surprised how often it tends to be overlooked.

2. Profitability

A higher volume of sales does not necessarily mean higher profits. This is again a fairly obvious point, though it is sometimes learned the hard way. I know of a craft operation with sales in the area of a quarter of a million dollars. The owner confessed recently to me that the after tax profit is actually less than what it was when he worked on his own and sold $50,000 worth of products in a year.

3. Lifestyle

A business with employees is substantially different from one where you work entirely on your own or with members of your family. Besides the additional complications of dealing with employees and the extra paperwork, there is a certain loss of privacy when you have hired workers on the premises. As well, some craftspeople feel that by enlarging their business the commercial side overshadows the creative side of their operation.

4. The market

Will expansion mean selling more products in the same market or will you have to open up new markets perhaps further afield? Remember the point made earlier about not approaching saturation in any given market area. As the volume sold in a given market area increases, it will eventually reach a point where the product begins to lose its appeal because there is simply too much in that market. There are very few handcrafted products to which this would not apply, although the saturation point is naturally different for different products.

It is possible to have a really "hot" product with a very high saturation point. Instead of saturation, the risk is that you will not produce enough and competitors will enter the field. If this is the case, then a careful plan of expansion may be the best course for you to follow.

5. Quality

If you make much larger quantities, you must ensure that the quality remains high. You must motivate your employees to produce according to your own exacting professional standards. You must have ways of monitoring and controlling quality.

b. FORECASTING

If you are planning to expand your craft business, you should prepare an operating forecast to see what will happen to your income and your costs. Generally a forecast is done for a one-year period, though you could choose a longer or a shorter period if you wish.

A forecast need not be a terribly complex affair. What you do is simply set out what you reasonably expect to happen to your revenue and expenses if certain changes take place.

A forecast can be of benefit to you in several ways. It can help you distinguish between the various alternatives open to you — to put up a new workshop or renovate and enlarge the old building, to hire additional employees and other decisions which will affect the future of your business. For example, you might discover a steadily increasing trend of retail sales from your own studio. You may not have paid too much attention to these because they were a relatively small percentage of your total sales. You might now want to consider setting up a separate retail outlet apart from your studio and possibly carry the work of other craftspeople as well as your own.

A forecast also forces you to look ahead and consider the overall financial position of your business. You may become aware of opportunities and concerns that are not apparent in the day-to-day operation of the business.

Suppose you find that despite an increase in sales, profits have been declining. You will then want to look very carefully at your expenses to see which of these has been showing a tendency to increase.

c. PREPARING THE FORECAST

When you prepare a forecast, you must think carefully about what your business can reasonably be expected to do. Be totally realistic. Naturally you *hope* for big increases in sales. But, when doing your forecast, you have to be guided by *reasonable expectations based on past results*. Start with your last year's operating statement. Then determine all the changes you plan to make and the effects these changes will have on your revenues, expenses, and profits.

Suppose you are planning to purchase a more expensive loom and hire an employee to work with you. These changes will mean a substantial increase in output, but the increase won't materialize right away. However, your expenses will increase immediately.

You are currently selling all the work you can produce, and yearly sales are about $50,000. You anticipate sales of about $100,000 on the basis of the following: your sales doubled last year over the previous year and your business is still in the early stages of growth; you are getting a lot of repeat orders; you expect more orders from a major trade show at which you plan to exhibit; you have just hired a sales representative; the general economic picture is beginning to look better than it has for some time.

Samples #13 and #14 show how your operating statement for the current year and your forecast for the following year might look.

SAMPLE #13
OPERATING STATEMENT

For the Year Ending Dec. 31, 198-

SALES	$50,000	
Raw materials	12,500	
Wages (paid to yourself)	12,500	
Gross profit		25,000
EXPENSES		
Accounting	500	
Advertising and shows	700	
Depreciation	800	
Electricity and fuel	1,200	
Freight	600	
Insurance	1,400	
Interest	3,200	
Miscellaneous	500	
Operating supplies	500	
Repairs	250	
Telephone	600	
Truck	2,000	
		12,250
Net profit		12,750

SAMPLE #14
OPERATING FORECAST

For the Year Ending Dec. 31, 198-

SALES		100,000
Raw materials	25,000	
Wages (yours plus employees')	25,000	
Gross profit		50,000
EXPENSES		
Accounting	500	
Advertising and shows	2,100	
Depreciation	2,000	
Electricity and fuel	1,800	
Freight	1,200	
Insurance	2,200	
Interest	4,000	
Miscellaneous	1,000	
Operating supplies	600	
Repairs	300	
Sales commissions	10,500	
Telephone	800	
Truck	2,400	
		29,400
Net profit		20,600

If you are convinced that expansion will mean increased profitability and you are prepared for the lifestyle changes that expansion usually brings, you have to consider the means by which you can carry out your expansion plans. If you plan to invest in a larger building and/or new tools and equipment, you have to arrange financing (see chapter 11). You will have to hire and train people to work for you (see chapter 16). You may have to open up new markets for your products (see chapters 5 to 7).

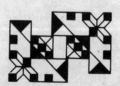

16

EMPLOYEES:
HOW TO HIRE AND TRAIN THEM

a. DO YOU NEED TO HIRE ANYONE?

As a general rule, you should not employ anyone in your craft business until you absolutely have to. The only exception to this is when you hire your spouse or children to help out. Before hiring anyone else, you should first look at the situation very carefully to be sure that it is really necessary. Perhaps you can reorganize your work, hire your spouse to do the bookkeeping, or speed up aspects of the work process.

Becoming an employer can radically change the nature of your business in a number of ways. When you hire employees, you become involved in many complex rules and regulations. There are laws governing hours of labor, minimum wages, and working conditions. You are obliged to collect payroll taxes. There are more government forms to fill out. Unless you are very fortunate in finding someone already qualified, you will have to invest time and money in training. Moreover, you may go to all the trouble of training someone only to have that person quit just after he or she has finished the training. Or your ex-employee may promptly go and set up a business in competition with yours.

However, most of these problems can be minimized if you go about the business of hiring in a systematic and clear-headed way. There is an absolute upper limit on what you can produce yourself. If you use hired help, you can greatly increase your output. You can delegate some of the more routine jobs to others and concentrate your own efforts on those tasks that call for the highest levels of skill. By freeing yourself from production in this way you can also spend more time on design and marketing. You can frequently produce a higher quality product by producing in quantity.

b. HIRING NEW EMPLOYEES

If it is possible to hire trained workers, then you won't have to worry about training. In most cases, however, you will have to spend time training new employees. Most craft businesses produce a product which, even if it is not really unique, is so highly specialized that it is difficult to find workers who can produce it without at least some training.

Naturally you would look for people with some previous training or experience in your own craft field. If you are a potter, you'd look for someone with at least a modicum of experience in pottery. If you are a metalworker, you'd look for someone with metalwork knowledge, and so on.

Training someone new is expensive. You will be obliged to pay a novice the minimum wage or a wage that is comparable to the prevailing wage rates in your area. In the beginning, the new person will probably not produce enough salable work to pay his or her wages. In some cases, it is possible to get federal and state or provincial aid to train new employees, but the paperwork requirements for most government training programs are frequently so complicated that it is not worthwhile.

Training is also time-consuming. Your output will be less initially because of the time you have to spend training the new employee. This can be offset to some extent by having the new person perform the more routine production tasks like loading the kiln, or nonproduction tasks like packing orders or taking inventory.

Many problems can be avoided if care is taken in the initial selection and hiring process. Don't rush out and hire the first person who is willing to work for you. A bad employee can make your life miserable and jeopardize the success of your business. Always look at more than one candidate for the job. Have a system of screening applicants. Don't just ask a job applicant to come talk to you about work until you have first prepared yourself.

Be sure that you know exactly what you want the employee to do and what kind of employee you want. Always ask prospective employees to fill out an application, giving their educational qualifications and past job experience. Get the names and addresses of previous employers and call or write them for references. If you are likely to be hiring a number of employees, it is worthwhile drawing up a reference form. You can photocopy this and send it to former employers.

Ask previous employers to confirm the information given to you by the job applicant; the nature of the employee's duties while in their service; the reason why the employee left their service; whether they would rehire the person; their assessment of the person's ability to handle the job he or she is applying for; the applicant's ability to get along with others and willingness to accept supervision. You might also ask them to rate the applicant (excellent, average, poor) in a number of specific categories: job performance, personality, neatness, attendance, and loyalty.

From the written applications, you should select the most promising candidates for an interview. Many craftspeople find job interviewing extremely difficult. Part of the reason is that they launch into it without sufficient preparation.

Jot down beforehand questions that you want to ask the candidate at the interview. During the interview, be as relaxed as possible and try to establish a comfortable, pleasant atmosphere. Be prepared to answer the candidate's questions about the nature of the job, pay, etc., but make sure that you retain control over the interview. Avoid a stand-offish, patronizing attitude, but at the same time make it clear that the applicant is the person being evaluated.

After the initial interview, select the most promising two or three candidates and invite them to a second interview. Devise a simple, practical test for them involving some kind of work in your workshop. Obviously, this test depends on their skill level and experience. If they have previous experience, let them have a go at the wheel, or the lathe, or the sewing machine. If they are beginners, give them something very simple. Your objective is to find out their *aptitude* for the work and to determine how conscientious they are.

There are no surefire, 100% successful methods for selecting a good employee. When you have assembled all the relevant facts, you have to apply your own individual judgment. Is the person likely to be a good worker? Is he or she the kind of person you want to have around you? After all, it's your business and you want to work in a pleasant and relaxed atmosphere. You don't want hassles and tension in the workplace.

A new employee should be hired for a trial period of about six months. This is usually long enough for you to decide if you want to keep an employee. If there are going to be problems with the employee's work habits or attitude toward the job, these should become apparent before the end of the trial period.

Don't think that all of this is too much trouble. If you are serious about expanding your business, your success will depend to a large extent on your ability to recruit, train, and *keep* good, reliable, and honest employees. If you hire carelessly, you are only asking for trouble. A bungling, disgruntled or dishonest employee can poison the work atmosphere, eat into the profits of your business, and destroy your peace of mind.

c. PAYING YOUR EMPLOYEES

There are several different ways of going about paying employees in a craft business. You can pay your employees a fixed salary, an hourly wage, a piece rate or some combination of these.

1. Salaries

If you have just one or two employees, you can pay them a fixed salary for a work week of a certain agreed upon number of hours. (The hourly equivalent must, of course, be at least equal to the legal minimum wage for your state or province.) Obviously, you must be sure that the employee's weekly output is sufficient and that it is consistent.

2. Wages

The most common payment method is an hourly wage, paid weekly. How much you will have to offer more experienced workers will depend on the prevailing wage rates in your community. If you are to keep costs under control, you must figure out just how much work per hour you produce and set a reasonable standard for a new employee.

One of the most difficult aspects of the transition from a one-person craft business to a business with employees is in the area of cost control. There is no problem in controlling labor costs if you are doing all the work yourself. If you have employees, you must watch your labor costs continually.

3. Piece rates

Paying your employees so much per piece is an excellent way of keeping the lid on costs. It does require a bit more paperwork and, in the beginning at least, a lot of calculations in order to determine just how much to pay for each and every article that you are making. You must work with an hourly equivalent in mind and do your calculations so that a reasonably efficient *trained* employee will make about the same that you would have to pay on an hourly basis.

The difference between an hourly rate and a piece rate system is that, having once worked out a set of piece rates, you will have automatic control of your labor costs. You also have a built-in incentive scheme, which will provide higher rewards to those workers who put forth a greater effort. You will, however, have to monitor the quality of work very carefully. But if the rates you set are realistic in terms of what your employees are capable of producing, quality need not suffer under a piece rate system.

Even if you are paying your employees on a piece rate basis, you will still have to pay hourly rates to people who are in training. Most new employees would not earn enough on a piece rate basis to meet minimum wage requirements. It is possible to have hourly rates of pay for trainees and a piece rate system for fully trained workers. However, you have to structure the piece rates so that there is an attractive differential between them and the hourly rates you pay a trainee. With a piece rate system, a good employee can earn more than he or she would under an hourly system.

d. PROFIT SHARING

Profit sharing has been used as an incentive to productivity in all kinds and sizes of business. It can work with piece rates or an hourly wage system. By setting aside a certain proportion of profits (say 20%) for distribution among your employees, you can give them a sense of participation in the business and the feeling of working together as a team.

e. COTTAGE INDUSTRY

There is a way to greatly increase output without actually hiring employees to come and work in your workshop. You can farm out work to people who produce, usually part-time, in their own homes. Many production crafts lend themselves particularly well to this "cottage industry" approach. There are many people who want to work part-time at home, doing something they like. Starting a business wouldn't interest them, but they would welcome the opportunity to earn some extra cash doing pleasant work in their spare time.

The cottage industry approach has a number of advantages. If you do not control the hours and conditions of labor of the people who produce for you, so that they are not legally your employees, you are not involved with the mass of rules and regulations pertaining to employees. Your overhead costs are much less with a cottage system. You do not need to invest as much money in building, tools, and equipment as you would if you had employees working with your tools under your own roof.

However, there are limitations to the cottage industry approach. It generally works best where the craft skills required are readily available in the community so extensive training is not required. If, for example, there is a strong tradition of quilt-making in an area, these skills could be used either directly in a quilt-making operation or in making related products, such as patchwork clothing. However, there are numerous successful cottage industries where the workers are first trained in the employer's workshop before they start producing at home.

You have much less control over the quantity of output with this type of operation. If the home producer is bound by formal agreement to produce certain quantities or to work certain hours, the tax department may want to consider him or her an employee and you will in effect lose many of the advantages of a cottage industry. While you may not have a formal, written agreement, it is possible for you to have an understanding with the person producing at home so it is mutually understood that a certain amount of work will be produced. However, there are some gray areas here. Before getting too deeply involved with a cottage industry you should first check, or ask your lawyer to check, whether there are any state or provincial laws which might affect your relationship with the home producers.

Quality control also requires special attention in a cottage industry situation. If work is being produced in your workshop, you can detect mistakes more quickly and avoid having a lot of rejects or seconds produced. An outworker may produce a week's work or more before faults are discovered. There is no infallible system to prevent this from happening. But the risk can be reduced greatly by making sure that your home producers are conscientious, careful workers to begin with, by giving them proper training, and by having a system of quality control checks on all work as soon as it is received.

There is also some risk in the cottage industry approach that your designs or production techniques will be copied and used to produce work that is sold to someone else or sold directly by the worker. The chances of this happening can be reduced if you are careful to select honest, reliable people and you know their motivation in wanting to work at home.

It is of course possible to combine a cottage industry system with one where you have employees who come in to work. Some makers of production crafts have all their more complex pieces done in the workshop and put the simpler, straightforward work out.

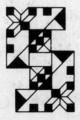

17

SOME TIPS
FOR CONTINUED SUCCESS

a. MAKE YOUR OWN DECISIONS

How big do you want your business to be? Do you want to hire people to work for you? These are questions involving major decisions that shape the future of your business. In the daily running of your business, there are many other decisions you'll have to make. Is the Sam Slick Gift Shop in the town of Haliburton a good credit risk? Should you use that new dye the salesperson said was so good? Which of the two sewing machines you've looked at is the better buy?

Decision-making is not just something that you'll have to do at crucial points in your business career. It is part of the day-to-day running of your business. Most decisions are basically simple. You add up all the pros and cons for each possible course of action and choose the best one.

This works in most cases. But what if you have looked thoroughly at all the advantages and disadvantages of alternative A and all the advantages and disadvantages of alternative B and neither emerges clearly as the best choice? The reasons for selecting A may be just as good as the reasons for selecting B.

There is a natural tendency in such situations to want to do nothing at all or to procrastinate as long as possible. You should resist this tendency at all costs. If you are trying to decide which of two apparently good opportunities is the best, procrastination could well cause you to miss both of them.

If after weighing up all the possibilities in a given situation, no clear choice emerges and you are unable to make a decision based on external, objective factors, you must then use your intuition, your gut feelings, your natural instincts or whatever you want to call it.

Some businesspeople will say that they make all their decisions according to their feelings. Don't believe them. Most successful business moves depend on rational calculation. But when all is said and done, there is usually room for a measure of feeling or intuition in many decisions.

As a businessperson, you are a decision-maker. It's not always easy. But you must learn to accept the role and avoid shying away from decisions, especially the difficult ones where clear choices don't appear to exist.

b. WHEN YOU NEED HELP, ASK FOR IT

Don't forget to ask for help if you need it. Whether you are trying to solve a technical problem, set up a marketing system, locate a supplier or tackle any of a hundred and one problems, there are others in the same boat as you. Use the resources of your local, national or regional crafts organization, seek advice from other craftspeople or explore your public library.

In the final analysis, you must make your own decision. But before you do so, get the best possible information you can. Never be afraid to ask a question or even to ask a favor. Most people are flattered when you seek their help, and they will do their best to oblige you.

Librarians can be especially helpful. After all, it's part of their job. You can get an immense amount of information from your public library on many craft subjects. Books on specific crafts can provide the answers to technical questions such as how to fasten two pieces of metal together, how to achieve a certain finish on the outside of your pots or what kind of preservative to use on your woodwork. You can locate the names and addresses of suppliers of raw materials or tools and equipment using the industrial and commercial directories that every good library has in its reference section. If you don't find what you want, ask a librarian.

c. BE THOROUGHLY PROFESSIONAL

To be successful in your craft business you must be thoroughly professional. Accept nothing less than the highest standards in your work. Never cut corners to produce work by a certain deadline. Plan ahead as far as possible and allow yourself sufficient time to fill the orders you take. Don't take on more work than you can handle. The goodwill of your customers is one of your most valuable possessions. Don't jeopardize it by being late in delivering or by shipping work that is not high quality.

d. LOOK AFTER DETAILS

A lot of the work of running a small business involves organization: organizing your time, planning your work, and planning your time off. If you adopt the attitude that only the big decisions are important and the little details will look after themselves, you're likely to end up a failure. Success in business depends on your ability to look after the details. But don't, on the other hand, become so bogged down in details that you can't see any longer where you are going.

e. KNOW WHEN TO DELEGATE

In the beginning of your business career you have to do everything yourself. You may build your own workshop, make all your products, get all the orders for your work, wrap your products, ship them to the customers, clean the floor, do the books, etc., etc. Later on, as your business grows, you may have people working for you and you can concentrate your energies where they are best used in your business.

But if this is to work properly, you must be able to delegate work to others. This is one of the hardest things for many craftspeople to do. There is an almost natural tendency to believe that only you can do the job right. In our business, we had to "educate" ourselves to accept the fact that others could actually be trained to produce our toys and turn them out as well as we could. But once we made this miraculous discovery, we were able to concentrate our own efforts on design, marketing, and quality control to make an even better product.

If you expand your business and hire people to work for you, your success will depend upon your ability to train and motivate your employees. To do this properly, you must have control at all times over costs and over the quality of your products. No matter how big your business grows, you must never let anything out of your workshop unless it is worthy of your own high professional standards. You can and must delegate work to others, but the ultimate responsibility for everything rests in your hands.

f. NEVER STOP LEARNING

No matter how far you go in your craft business, there is always more to learn about your craft and about business. You can learn from people, from books, and from experimenting on your own. A useful habit is to carry a small notebook with you and to jot down ideas as they occur to you. Be constantly on the lookout for new product ideas, new techniques, and new materials that you can use. Whenever you travel, look into craft and gift shops and check products and prices. Frequently you'll see a product being sold in another part of the country that you can make or make in a modified form. Sometimes one of your customers may have a suggestion that you can turn into a money-making product.

Keep your eyes open for new market opportunities. The craft field is so incredibly flexible that it would be pointless to try to list all possible market opportunities. One craftsperson I know is making all kinds of money producing custom furniture for institutions and offices. Another is doing a healthy business supplying props for store windows. There are plenty of opportunities out there if you are prepared to use your imagination and put in a little hard work.

g. YOUR LEISURE TIME

Plan your time off wisely. If you are your own boss, you can also be your own worst enemy, subject to the mercy of your own whims and caprices. You can spend a lot of time goofing off or go to the opposite extreme and work yourself half to death.

There are critical times in the life of every business when extraordinary effort and longer than average hours are called for. But if you find yourself permanently on a treadmill, then you are doing something wrong. Perhaps you need to hire an assistant, get someone part-time to do the bookkeeping or reorganize your work schedule. A well-run craft business should leave you sufficient time to enjoy other aspects of life.

A craft business does provide the opportunity to do away with the sharp distinction between work and play. For many people work is an unpleasant necessity they want to get over with as quickly as possible so that they can begin "living." If you are working at something you like, you can abolish this distinction and achieve true contentment, enjoying both your work and your time off.

But if you are in this fortunate position, *don't* forget to take time off. Even if you are in love with your work, you need holidays at regular intervals. You need to renew your energies, to rest your mind and body, and to share other aspects of human experience. Also, and very importantly, there is your family to consider. If they're not happy and contented, you won't be, and if you're not reasonably happy, life is not worthwhile no matter how much money you are making.

Look at your craft business as a profession that provides you with some rather unique lifestyle advantages. It can bring you a good income doing something you like as well as a good measure of leisure time if you organize it properly. The chapter on production advocated controlling the size of your inventory with several factors in mind. I suggested keeping some extra inventory ready so you could handle orders during the peak season when you were busy invoicing and selling and unable to devote very much time to production.

In our business, we take this one step further and build our inventory up so that we can take a good long summer vacation and go sailing. A lot of orders come in during the summer tourist season so we build up a large inventory in the early spring. During the summer, we go to the workshop one or two days a week to pack and ship the orders and do the paperwork. It costs us a little extra to build up our inventory so high in the spring, but it is worth it for the extra leisure time it makes possible during the warm summer months.

There are plenty of ways you can vary your working hours to suit your own particular lifestyle. You may choose to work on the weekends and take a couple of days off in the middle of the week to escape the weekend crowds. Or you may prefer to work all summer and take your vacation at the end of the season when the tourist rush is over.

The key to a high return from your craft business is to choose the mix of salary, profit, and leisure that brings you the highest degree of satisfaction. If you are facing a difficult period, you may have to work harder and put in more hours than usual. But once your business is established, you have the opportunity to take your rewards in the form of increased leisure as well as profits.

h. CAN YOU LICENSE YOUR HANDCRAFTED PRODUCT?

Some very interesting new possibilities for craftspeople have emerged in connection with the recent tremendous popularity of licensed products. The importance of licensed products has grown astronomically in the past five years. Last year in the United States, licensed products accounted for $20 billion in sales. In Canada, sales were approximately $2 billion.

Traditionally, licensing has attracted a high degree of attention in the areas of toys, children's wear, and juvenile merchandise. But in recent years, it has spread to many other areas, including clothing of all kinds, housewares, pottery, and jewelry.

Until quite recently, most successful licensed products came from movies, cartoons, and television. The character E.T. is perhaps the best example. Today, more and more licensed products do not spring from the entertainment industry but from other origins. Some are the result of a drawing board concept that is developed and marketed according to a calculated licensing program. Others have their origins in the craft world, and have been made into huge commercial successes by large North American manufacturers with computerized assembly lines producing individualized, one-of-a-kind products.

Some craftspeople are appalled by the idea of using a computerized assembly line to produce simulated handcrafts. They argue that such products can never attain the *quality* of real handcrafted goods. Others see the new production techniques as a step into the postindustrial society of the future, an opportunity to make high quality, unique products available to a wide market.

But there is no argument over the tremendous appeal of handcrafted products today. In this context, licensing offers the craftsperson a means of making his or her work widely available. If a craftsperson has designed and made a highly successful product that appears to have a wide market appeal — far beyond the limits of an individual's production capacity — it may be possible to license others to produce the product in return for a royalty fee based on a certain percentage of sales.

While the returns from licensing can be highly lucrative, the field is fraught with risks. There are huge promotional, advertising, and legal expenses. The growth of the licensing field has spawned a new type of professional — the licensing agent. This individual or company acts as a go-between for manufacturers and the licensor. If you think that your handcrafted product has licensing possibilities, it may be worth talking to a licensing agent. Two trade magazines, *The Licensing Letter* and the *Merchandising Reporter*, can provide more information on licensing.

APPENDIX 1

CRAFT ORGANIZATIONS/AGENCIES

It is not feasible in a book of this size to provide a comprehensive list of all craft organizations in the U.S. and Canada. Some of the most active craft groups are local or regional. Others are organized on the basis of a specific craft, e.g., weaving or pottery. The larger urban organizations are listed in local telephone directories. Others can be located by contacting the larger state and/or provincial groups or agencies listed below.

UNITED STATES

ALABAMA

Alabama State Council on the Arts
449 S. McDonough
Montgomery, AL 36130

Northeast Alabama Craftsmen's
Association
Box 1113, West Station
Huntsville, AL 35807

ALASKA

Ketchikan Arts and Craft Guild
Western Arts and Crafts Guild
Box 6572
Ketchikan, AK 99901

ARIZONA

Arts Community Association of
Arizona
Box 416000
Tucson, AZ 85717

ARKANSAS

Arkansas State Arts and Humanities
Continental Building, Suite 500
Markham and Main
Little Rock, AR 72201

CALIFORNIA

Santa Cruz Association of Artists and
Craftspeople
1001 Center Street
Santa Cruz, CA 95060

COLORADO

National Carvers Museum
Foundation
Woodcarver Road
Monument, CO 80132

CONNECTICUT

Handweavers' Guild of America
Box 7-374, 65 La Salle Road
West Hartford, CT 06107

DELAWARE

Delaware Art Museum
Education Dept.
2301 Kentmere Parkway
Wilmington, DE 19806

FLORIDA

Department of Crafts Design
Florida State University
Tallahassee, FL 32305

GEORGIA

Georgia Designer Craftsmen, Inc.
135 W. Wieuca Road N.W.
Atlanta, GA 30342

IDAHO

Idaho Commission on the Arts and
Humanities
c/o Statehouse
304 W. State Street
Boise, ID 83720

INDIANA

Indiana Arts Commission
155 E. Market Street
Indianapolis, IN 46204

IOWA

Iowa Designer Craftsmen
513 Nebraska Street
Sioux City, IA 51101

KENTUCKY

Kentucky Arts Commission
100 W. Main Street
Frankfort, KY 40601

Southern Kentucky Guild of Artists
and Craftsmen, Inc.
Box 1874
Bowling Green, KY 42101

LOUISIANA

Louisiana Crafts Council
139 Broadway
New Orleans, LA 70118

MAINE

Maine State Commission on the Arts
and the Humanities
State House
Augusta, ME 04333

MASSACHUSETTS

The Society of North American
Goldsmiths
591 Washington Street
Wellesley, MA 02181

MICHIGAN

Michigan Council for the Arts
1200 6th Avenue
Detroit, MI 48226

MISSISSIPPI

Mississippi Gulf Coast Craftsmen's
Guild, Inc.
Box 58
Gulfport, MS 39501

NEBRASKA

Nebraska Arts Council
8448 W. Center Road
Omaha, NE 68124

NEW HAMPSHIRE

League of New Hampshire Craftsmen
205 N. Main Street
Concord, NH 03301

New Hampshire Commission on the
Arts
40 N. Main Street
Concord, NH 03301

NEW JERSEY

New Jersey State Council on the Arts
109 W. State Street
Trenton, NJ 08608

NEW YORK

American Council for the Arts
570 7th Avenue
New York, NY 10018

American Craft Council
401 Park Avenue S.
New York, NY 10019

NORTH CAROLINA

North Carolina Arts Council
Dept. of Cultural Resources
Raleigh, NC 27611

OHIO

Ohio Arts Council
50 W. Broad Street, Suite 3600
Columbus, OH 43227

OKLAHOMA

Oklahoma Arts and Humanities
Council
640 Jim Thorpe Building
Oklahoma City, OK 73105

OREGON

Oregon Arts Commission
835 Summer Street N.E.
Salem, OR 97301

SOUTH DAKOTA

South Dakota Arts Council
108 W. 11th Street
Sioux Falls, SD 57102

TEXAS

Texas Commission on the Arts and
Humanities
Box 13406
Capitol Station
Austin, TX 78711

VERMONT

Vermont Council on the Arts, Inc.
136 State Street
Montpelier, VT 05602

Craft Professionals of Vermont
Rt. 1
West Burke, VT 05871

VIRGINIA

Commission of Arts and Humanities
400 E. Grace Street, 1st Floor
Richmond, VA 23219

Virginia Crafts Council
717 Rugby Road
Charlottesville, VA 22903

WASHINGTON

Arts Council of the Mid-Columbia
Region
Box 735
Richland, WA 99352

WEST VIRGINIA

West Virginia Department of
Culture and History
Arts and Humanities Division
Science and Culture Center
Capitol Complex
Charleston, VA 25305

WISCONSIN

Wisconsin Arts Board
123 W. Washington Avenue
Madison, WI 53702

CANADA

ALBERTA

Arts and Crafts Society of Alberta
10998 126th Street
Edmonton, AB T5M 0P5

BRITISH COLUMBIA

Craftsmen's Association of
British Columbia
1411 Cartwright Street
Granville Island
Vancouver, B.C. V6H 3R7

MANITOBA

Crafts Guild of Manitoba
183 Kennedy Street
Winnipeg, MB R3G 1S6

NEW BRUNSWICK

New Brunswick Crafts Council
Box/C.P. 1231
Fredericton, NB E3B 5C8

NEWFOUNDLAND

Newfoundland and Labrador
Crafts Development Association
P.O. Box 5295
St. John's, NF A1C 5W1

NOVA SCOTIA

Nova Scotia Designer Craftsmen
Box 3355 South
Halifax, NS B3J 3J1

ONTARIO

Canadian Crafts Council
#16, 46 Elgin Street
Ottawa, ON K1P 5K6

Ontario Crafts Council
346 Dundas Street W.
Toronto, ON M5T 1G5

PRINCE EDWARD ISLAND

Prince Edward Island Craftsmen's
Council
Box 1573
Charlottetown, PEI C1A 1N0

QUEBEC

Guilde Canadienne de Metiers d'Art
2025 Peel Street
Montreal, PQ H3A 1T6

SASKATCHEWAN

Saskatchewan Arts Board
200 Lakeshore Drive
Regina, SK S4P 3V7

APPENDIX 2

GOVERNMENT DEVELOPMENT AGENCIES IN THE UNITED STATES AND CANADA

There are great variations in the amount and kind of state or provincial assistance available to small businesses, including craft businesses. Some states and provinces have special small business development programs, a few have special programs for craft businesses. To find out more about the kind of assistance available to craft businesses in your state or province, you should write to your state or provincial development agency.

UNITED STATES

ALABAMA

Alabama Development Office
c/o State Capitol
3734 Atlanta Highway
Montgomery, AL 36130

ALASKA

Commissioner
Department of Commerce and
Economic Development
Pouch D
Juneau, AK 99811

ARIZONA

Arizona Office of Economic Planning
and Development
1700 W. Washington
Phoenix, AZ 85007

ARKANSAS

Executive Director
Department of Economic
Development
One Capitol Mill
Little Rock, AR 72201

CALIFORNIA

Director
Department of Economic and
Business Development
P.O. Box 1499
Sacramento, CA 95805

COLORADO

Director
Division of Commercial and Economic
Development
500 State Centennial Building
Denver, CO 80203

CONNECTICUT

Commissioner
Connecticut Department of Economic
Development
210 Washington Street
Hartford, CT 06106

DELAWARE

Director
Delaware Department of Community
Affairs and Economic Development
630 State College Road
P.O. Box 1401
Dover, DE 19901

DISTRICT OF COLUMBIA

Director
Office of Business and Economic
Development
DC Building, Room 201
1350 East Street, N.W.
Washington, DC 20004

FLORIDA

Chief
Division of Economic Development
Florida Department of Commerce
107 West Gaines Street
Tallahassee, FL 32301

GEORGIA

Commissioner
Georgia Department of Industry and
Trade
1400 North DMNI International
Atlanta, GA 30303

HAWAII

Hawaii Department of Planning
and Economic Development
Kamamula Building
250 South King Street
Honolulu, HI 96804

IDAHO

Administrator
Division of Tourism and Industrial
Development
Capitol Building
Boise, ID 83720

ILLINOIS

Director
Illinois Department of Commercial
and Community Affairs
222 South College
Springfield, IL 62706

INDIANA

Executive Director
Indiana Department of Commerce
440 North Meridian Street
Indianapolis, IN 46220

IOWA

Director
Iowa Development Commission
250 Jewett Building
Des Moines, IA 50309

KANSAS

Secretary
Kansas Department of Economic
Development
503 Kansas Avenue
Topeka, KS 66603

KENTUCKY

Commissioner
Kentucky Department of Commerce
Capital Plaza Towers
Frankfort, KY 40601

LOUISIANA

Director of Economic Development
Louisiana Department of Commerce
P.O. Box 44185
Baton Rouge, LA 70804

MAINE

Director
State Development Office
193 State Street
Augusta, ME 04333

MARYLAND

Secretary
Maryland Department of Economic
and Community Development
Office of Business and Industrial
Development
1748 Forest Drive
Annapolis, MD 21401

MASSACHUSETTS

Secretary
Massachusetts Department of
Commerce and Development
100 Cambridge Street
Boston, MA 02202

MICHIGAN

Director
Office of Economic Development
Michigan Department of Commerce
P.O. Box 30225
Lansing, MI 48909

MINNESOTA

Commissioner
Department of Economic
Development
Hanover Building
480 Cedar Street
St. Paul, MN 55101

MISSISSIPPI

Director
Mississippi Department of Economic
Development
P.O. Box 849
1202 State Office Building
Jackson, MS 39205

MISSOURI

Director
Division of Commercial and Economic
Development
1014 Madison Street
Jefferson City, MO 65102

MONTANA

Director
Office of Commerce and Small
Business Development
State Capital Building
Helena, MT 59601

NEBRASKA

Director
Nebraska Department of Economic
Development
P.O. Box 94666
301 Centennial Mall South
Lincoln, NE 68509

NEVADA

Director
Nevada Department of Economic
Development
Capitol Complex
Carson City, NV 89710

NEW HAMPSHIRE

Commissioner
Department of Resources and
Economic Development
P.O. Box 856
Concord, NH 03301

NEW JERSEY

Director
Division of Economic Development
Department of Labor and Industry
P.O. Box 2766
Trenton, NJ 08625

NEW MEXICO

Existing Industries Liaison
Economic Development Division
Department of Commerce and
Industry
Bataan Memorial Building
Santa Fe, NM 87503

NEW YORK

Commissioner
Department of Commerce
99 Washington Avenue
Albany, NY 12245

NORTH CAROLINA

Executive Director
Business Assistance Division
North Carolina Department of
Commerce
430 N. Salisbury Street, Suite 294
Raleigh, NC 27611

NORTH DAKOTA

Director
Business and Industrial Development
Department
513 E. Bismarck Avenue
Bismarck, ND 58505

OHIO

Director
Department of Economic and
Community Development
30 E. Broad Street, 25th Floor
Columbus, OH 43215

OKLAHOMA

Director
Industrial Development Department
Office of the Governor
Oklahoma City, OK 73105

OREGON

Director
Department of Economic
Development
155 Cottage Street N.E.
Salem, OR 97310

PENNSYLVANIA

Secretary
Pennsylvania Department of
Commerce
419 South Office Building
Harrisburg, PA 17120

RHODE ISLAND

Director
Rhode Island Department of
Economic Development
One Weybossett Hill
Providence, RI 02908

SOUTH CAROLINA

Director
South Carolina State Development
Board
P.O. Box 927
Columbia, SC 29202

SOUTH DAKOTA

Director
South Dakota IDEA
221 South Central
Pierre, SD 57501

TENNESSEE

Commissioner
Economic and Community
Development Division
1007 Andrew Jackson Building
Nashville, TN 37219

TEXAS

Executive Director
Texas Industrial Commission
Capital Station
Box 12728
410 E. Fifth Avenue
Austin, TX 78711

UTAH

Business Development Co-ordinator
Economic and Industrial
Development Division
2 Arrow Press Square
165 South West Temple
Salt Lake City, UT 84101

VERMONT

Commissioner of Economic
Development
Vermont Agency of Development
and Community Affairs
109 State Street
Montpelier, VT 05602

VIRGINIA

Director
Virginia Division Industrial
Development
1010 State Office Building
Richmond, VA 23219

WASHINGTON

Director
Department of Commercial and
Economic Development
101 General Administrative Building
Olympia, WA 98504

WEST VIRGINIA

Director
Governor's Office of Economic and
Community Development
State Capitol
Charleston, WV 25305

WISCONSIN

Secretary
Department of Business
Development
123 West Washington Avenue
Madison, WI 53702

WYOMING

Executive Director
Department of Economic Planning
and Development
Barrett Building
Cheyenne, WY 82002

PUERTO RICO

Deputy Administrator
Puerto Rico Economic Development
Administration
Continental Operations Branch
1290 Avenue of the Americas
New York, NY 10019

105

CANADA

ALBERTA

Alberta Tourism and Small Business
16th Floor
Capital Square Building
10065 Jasper Avenue
Edmonton, AB T5J 0H4

BRITISH COLUMBIA

Ministry of Industry and Small
Business Development
Parliament Buildings
Victoria, BC V8V 1X4

MANITOBA

Manitoba Culture, Heritage and
Recreation
177 Lombard Avenue
Winnipeg, MB R3B 0W5

NEW BRUNSWICK

New Brunswick Department of
Commerce and Development
Box 6000
Fredericton, NB E3B 5H1

NEWFOUNDLAND

Department of Development
Box 4750
St. John's, NF A1C 5T7

NOVA SCOTIA

Department of Development
P.O. Box 519
Halifax, NS B3J 2R7

ONTARIO

Ministry of Industry and Trade
900 Bay Street, Hearst Block
Queen's Park
Toronto, ON M7A 2E1

PRINCE EDWARD ISLAND

Department of Industry
Box 2000
Charlottetown, PEI C1A 7N8

QUEBEC

Department of Industry, Trade
and Tourism
1 Place Ville Marie
23rd Floor
Montreal, PQ H3B 3M6

SASKATCHEWAN

Department of Economic
Development and Trade
2103 11th Avenue
Regina, SK S4P 3V7

OTHER TITLES IN THE
SELF-COUNSEL BUSINESS SERIES

MARKETING YOUR PRODUCT
A planning guide for small business
Learn the secrets of successful product marketing. Marketing is not just selling and advertising; its objectives are to help you decide if you are developing the right product for the right target market, and if you are using the promotion vehicles and distribution methods to maximize the return on your efforts.

The in-depth checklists included in this book will take you, step by step, toward a successful, profitable marketing strategy. $12.95

Contents include:

- What is marketing?
- Marketing planning, goal-setting, and strategy
- Segmenting your market and identifying consumer behavior
- Researching your market
- Developing your product
- Pricing to sell
- Advertising
- Public relations
- Distribution: getting the product to your customer
- Retailing your product
- Selling as a marketing technique
- Legal considerations
- Marketing your product internationally
- Implementing the marketing plan
- Appendix - worksheets to develop your own strategy
- Glossary of terms

PREPARING A SUCCESSFUL BUSINESS PLAN
A practical guide for small business
At some time, every business needs a formal business plan. Whether considering a new business venture or rethinking an existing one, an effective plan is essential to success. From start to finish, this working guide outlines how to prepare a plan that will win potential investors and help achieve business goals.

Using worksheets and a sample plan, readers learn how to create an effective plan, establish planning and maintenance methods, and update their strategy in response to actual business conditions. $14.95

Contents include:

- The basic elements of business planning
- The company and its product
- The marketing plan
- The financial plan
- The team
- Concluding remarks and appendixes
- The executive summary
- Presenting an impressive document
- Common misconceptions in business planning
- Your business plan as a tangible asset

THE BUSINESS GUIDE TO PROFITABLE CUSTOMER RELATIONS
Today's techniques for success

You need good service to attract customers and keep them coming back, and this book provides plans and programs that have been proven successful by other businesses. No matter what kind of business you are in, this book will help increase profits through improved customer relations. $7.95

Contents include:

- Customer service — what it is and what it is not
- The "why" of customer relations
- The value of service
- Developing a profitable customer relations program
- Setting goals for your business
- Putting your plan together
- Communicating your customer relations program to your employees
- Training employees
- Bringing it all together

EVERY RETAILER'S GUIDE TO LOSS PREVENTION
Keep your profits! Stop theft!

If you are in business to make a profit, this book is for you! It covers planning and implementing a loss prevention program, training employees to spot and foil shoplifters, dealing with internal theft, identifying counterfeit currency, how to act during a robbery, and much more. The authors' proven techniques will help you make your retail business more secure and let you stop paying thieves out of your profits. $12.95

Contents include:

- Loss and loss prevention
- Shoplifting
- How to protect you and your store
- Markdowns, refunds, and cash handling
- Checks, credit cards, and fraud
- Counterfeit money
- Robbery
- Bomb threats, hostage takings, and kidnap
- Descriptions
- Internal theft
- The buyer/seller relationship
- Management techniques for loss prevention
- Arrest
- Attending court and giving evidence
- The professional store detective
- Developing and maintaining a loss prevention program

FINANCIAL CONTROL FOR THE SMALL BUSINESS

A practical primer for keeping a tighter rein on your profits and cash flow

Many small business people are frightened by the prospect of balancing ledgers, drawing up income statements and balance sheets, and comparing their current assets to their liabilities. However, this book takes the mystery out of accounting. In easy-to-understand language, this book takes you through the "after the basics" accounting procedure for the small business. $6.95

Contents include:

- An overview of accounting
- Financial statements
- Depreciation
- Income statement analysis
- Balance sheet analysis
- Internal control
- Cost management
- Fixed and variable costs
- Cost-volume-profit analysis
- Budgeting
- Cash management
- Long-term investments
- Leasing

BASIC ACCOUNTING FOR THE SMALL BUSINESS

Simple, foolproof techniques for keeping your books straight and staying out of trouble

Having bookkeeping problems? Do you feel you should know more about bookkeeping, but simply don't have time for a course? Do you wish that the paperwork in your business could be improved, but you don't know where or how to start?

This book is a down-to-earth manual on how to save your accountant's time and your time and money. Written in clear, everyday English, not in accounting jargon, this guide will help you and your office staff keep better records. U.S. edition $6.95, Canadian edition $7.95

Contents include:

- Your accountant
- On buying a business
- Sales, across the counter, in the mail
- Cash
- Receivables
- Payables
- The synoptic journal
- The general ledger
- Expenses
- The bank and you
- Payrolls
- Inventories
- Contents of a balance sheet
- What is "cash flow?"
- The general journal
- The trial balance
- The columnar work sheet
- Plus 30 samples of the various journals and financial statements

A PRACTICAL GUIDE TO FINANCIAL MANAGEMENT
Tips and and techniques for the non-financial manager

Good financial management is the key to high profits. It takes more than hard work and the right product to be successful in a small business. You must know how to manage your financial resources wisely and effectively. This book explains in easy-to-understand language how to get the most from every dollar you spend or save. It provides practical, realistic advice for those managers who do not have a background in finance, and it illustrates the many kinds of financial statements you should know how to draw up. $7.95

Contents inlcude:

- Financial ratio analysis
- Working capital management
- Cash budgeting
- Equity financing
- Debt financing
- Short-term financing
- Intermediate - and long-term financing
- Sources of funding
- Financial plan
- Long-term asset management
- Leasing
- 21 samples

ASSERTIVENESS FOR MANAGERS
Learning effective skills for managing people

Learn to deal more effectively with your employees, co-workers, and superiors. This book explains the uses of assertive skills and provides a step-by-step approach for learning the techniques that are most useful in the business world. Worksheets are included. $9.95

Contents include:

- Why do managers need assertive skills?
- What is assertive behavior?
- The basic "give" skills of assertive behavior
- The basic "take" skills of assertive behavior
- How give and take work together
- How to handle the poor performer
- Setting goals that work
- The manager as a career coach
- Assertiveness skills for women at work

A SMALL BUSINESS GUIDE TO EMPLOYEE SELECTION
Finding, interviewing, and hiring the right people

This book offers employers practical information on how to successfully select productive employees. It includes sample advertisements, application forms, suggested interview questions, and role-play exercises for the interviewer/applicant exchange. $6.95

READY-TO-USE BUSINESS FORMS
A complete package for the small business

Running a small business and keeping it in order can be made much simpler if efficient systems are in place and the paperwork is up to date. This handy guide of tear-out forms is just what your small business needs to help you take the worry out of daily record-keeping and routine tasks and put more time into keeping on top of your competitors. $10.95

THE BUSINESS WRITING WORKBOOK
A guide to defensive writing skills

This writing guide provides exercises and worksheets to practice skills that are directly applicable to anyone in a supervisory or management setting. $9.95

BUSINESS ETIQUETTE TODAY
A guide to corporate success

In this guide you will learn about table and party conversation, telephone talk, company protocol, keeping clients and colleagues waiting, and the new rules of behavior emerging as women and men find themselves at the same conference table. $7.95

CHAIRING A MEETING WITH CONFIDENCE
An easy guide to rules and procedure

The author uses everyday language to demystify the art of conducting a meeting in a fair, orderly, and efficient manner. This is not a rules book, but a simple guide on how to run a meeting according to the rules of order. Your meetings can become an effective tool in dealing with the business of the day and the venue for discussion that is productive and to the point. $7.95

THE BUSINESS GUIDE TO EFFECTIVE SPEAKING
Making presentations, using audio-visuals, and dealing with the media

Effective communication has always been the key to business success and this book provides a straightforward businesslike approach to developing and improving on-the-job speaking skills. $7.95

DESIGN YOUR OWN LOGO
A step-by-step guide for businesses, organizations and individuals

This handy book gives background information to the psychology of effective logos and includes a step-by-step guide to designing one for any purpose. $9.95

For information on how you can have *Better Homes & Gardens* magazine delivered to your door, write to: Robert Austin, P.O. Box 4536, Des Moines, IA 50336.

> $11.95   ISBN 0-88908-644-3   BPM

ORDER FORM

All prices are subject to change without notice. Books are available in book, department, and stationery stores, or use this order form. (Please print)

Name_____

Address_____

_____

Charge to:

❑Visa   ❑ MasterCard

Account Number_____

Validation Date _____

Expiry Date _____

Signature_____

❑**Check here for a free catalogue which outlines all of our publications.**

IN CANADA
Please send your order to the nearest location:

Self-Counsel Press
1481 Charlotte Road
North Vancouver, B. C.
V7J 1H1

Self-Counsel Press
2399 Cawthra Road, Unit 25
Mississauga, Ontario
L5A 2W9

IN THE U.S.A.
Please send your order to:

Self-Counsel Press Inc.
1704 N. State Street
Bellingham, WA 98225
YES, please send me:

_____copies of **Marketing Your Product,** $12.95

_____copies of **Preparing a Successful Business Plan,** $14.95

_____copies of **The Business Guide to Profitable Customer Relations,** $7.95

_____copies of **Every Retailer's Guide to Loss Prevention,** $12.95

_____copies of **Financial Control for the Small Business,** $6.95

_____copies of **Basic Accounting for the Small Business** U.S. edition. $6.95 Canadian edition, $7.95

_____copies of **A Practical Guide to Financial Management,** $7.95

_____copies of **Assertiveness for Managers,** $9.95

_____copies of **A Small Business Guide to Employee Selection,** $6.95

_____copies of **Ready-To-Use Business Forms,** $10.95

_____copies of **The Business Writing Workbook,** $9.95

_____copies of **Business Etiquette Today,** $7.95

_____copies of **Chairing a Meeting With Confidence,** $7.95

_____copies of **The Business Guide to Effective Speaking,** $7.95

_____copies of **Design Your Own Logo,** $9.95

Please add $2.50 for postage & handling.

WA residents, please add 7.8% sales tax.